A Portrait of Christ

A Portrait of Christ

A Look at Who Jesus Is and What He Is Like from the Gospels

D. Patrick Ramsey

RESOURCE *Publications* · Eugene, Oregon

A PORTRAIT OF CHRIST
A Look at Who Jesus Is and What He Is Like from the Gospels

Copyright © 2013 D. Patrick Ramsey. All rights reserved. Except for brief quotations in critical publications or reviews, no part of this book may be reproduced in any manner without prior written permission from the publisher. Write: Permissions, Wipf and Stock Publishers, 199 W. 8th Ave., Suite 3, Eugene, OR 97401.

Resource Publications
An Imprint of Wipf and Stock Publishers
199 W. 8th Ave., Suite 3
Eugene, OR 97401
www.wipfandstock.com

ISBN 13: 978-1-62032-768-5
Manufactured in the U.S.A.

Unless otherwise indicated, Scripture quotations are from the The Holy Bible, English Standard Version®, copyright © 2001 by Crossway Bibles, a publishing ministry of Good News Publishers. Used by permission. All rights reserved.

Scripture marked NKJV is taken from the New King James Version®. Copyright © 1982 by Thomas Nelson, Inc. Used by permission. All rights reserved.

Scripture marked NASB is taken from the New American Standard Bible®, Copyright © 1960, 1962, 1963, 1968, 1971, 1972, 1973,1975, 1977, 1995 by The Lockman Foundation. Used by permission.

Scripture quotations marked NLT are taken from the Holy Bible, New Living Translation, copyright © 1996, 2004, 2007 by Tyndale House Foundation. Used by permission of Tyndale House Publishers, Inc., Carol Stream, Illinois 60188. All rights reserved.

To my wife Rachel,
the delight of my eyes.

Jesus is God lived by a man.

—F. GODET

Contents

Preface   ix

1   The Promised Christ   1
2   The Divine-Human Savior   14
3   The Compassionate Christ   27
4   The Compassionate Christ, Part 2   36
5   Christ the Friend   45
6   The Anger of Christ   54
7   The Humility of Christ   62

Bibliography   71
Study Guide   73

Preface

THIS BOOK ORIGINATED AS a sermon series on the person of Jesus Christ. It focused on answering two questions, "Who is Jesus?" and "What is Jesus like?" The emphasis was decidedly on the second question and this is reflected in the book. I was especially helped in this regard by B. B. Warfield's article, "On the Emotional Life of Our Lord." It is indeed a classic and well worth reading today.

I would like to thank Dr. Michael Haykin of Southern Baptist Theological Seminary for reading the manuscript and for his helpful suggestions. I would also like to thank my wife, Rachel, and my five boys Sean, Drew, Aidan, Luke, and Asher for their continuing love and support. Most especially, I would like to thank Jesus, the subject of this book, for saving me from my sins and loving me with an everlasting love.

1

The Promised Christ

A NUMBER OF WELL-LOVED books share a common theme: an epic battle between good and evil. In *The Lord of the Rings*, for example, Aragorn and company wage war against the powerful but evil Sauron; and in *The Lion, the Witch and the Wardrobe*, Aslan the lion battles the White Witch.

These great stories also share a number of other elements that make them gripping and intriguing. One is that their battles have universal and grave consequences. If Frodo fails in his mission to destroy the ring, and if Aslan does not come to conquer the Witch, then all is lost for everyone. There is a do-or-die element to these stories.

Another common component is the oppression of people by an evil tyrant. Times are tough and desperate. In *The Lion, the Witch and the Wardrobe*, the citizens of Narnia live in constant fear of their ruler, the White Witch, who makes it winter all year round, but never Christmas. The story is somewhat different in *The Lord of the Rings*, as the evil Sauron is not quite in control of Middle Earth, but he is rapidly gaining strength and is on the brink of complete domination.

A Portrait of Christ

Still another theme, which binds together many of these well-loved stories, is the presence of a promised hero who will save the oppressed. This is especially the case in Lewis's *The Lion, the Witch and the Wardrobe*. Many of the Narnians have lived in hope for a very long time, because of the prophecy that one day the great and mighty Aslan will come to Narnia and right all wrongs and turn winter into spring. Aslan's victory, according to another prophecy, will happen when two daughters of Eve and two sons of Adam arrive in Narnia and sit on the four thrones at Cair Paravel. This is why when Mrs. Beaver meets Peter, Susan, Edmund, and Lucy for the very first time, she exclaims, "So you've come at last! At last! To think that ever I should live to see this day!"[1]

Good versus evil, oppression, deliverance, powerful enemies, promised saviors, and do-or-die battles are all components that wonderful epic stories have in common. Yet, there is something else they share: to one degree or another, they reflect reality. Perhaps this is why such stories are so popular. They express truth in the form of art, which we can relate to, and which we long to experience ourselves.

While we may be unaware of it, there has been a cosmic battle between good and evil since the time of Adam and Eve in the garden. Since the entrance of the first sin into the world, humanity has been enslaved and oppressed, subject to all sorts of misery, including death. Against this background, God has promised to send a savior to rescue his people.

The four Gospels teach that Jesus is this promised savior. Jesus of Nazareth, the son of Mary, is no ordinary man. He is the one the Old Testament prophets said would come to deliver God's people.

---

1. Lewis, *The Lion, the Witch and the Wardrobe*, 78.

The Need for a Savior

Evil first entered God's good universe when an angel opposed God and subsequently was cast out of heaven. The Bible tells us very little about the fall of Satan, but it does seem that pride was a root cause of his rebellion. Also, it is clear that he took many angels with him. Fallen or rebellious angels are commonly called demons.

In his hatred for God, Satan sought to destroy the apex of God's creation, human beings, who are made in the image of God. The evil one cunningly tempted the first two human beings, Adam and Eve, to rebel against God by eating the forbidden fruit (Genesis 3). Tragically, Satan was successful. Adam ate the fruit, bringing sin and its consequences into the world (Romans 5).

The situation in Narnia under the White Witch somewhat captures humankind's situation since Adam's fall into sin: living under an evil tyrant in a place where it is always winter and never Christmas. The Bible teaches that all men are by nature living under the tyrannical rule of Satan (Eph 2:2; 1 John 5:19). Furthermore, the Bible teaches that all humans are sinners, and are therefore under God's wrath and curse and are "liable to all miseries in this life, to death itself, and to the pains of hell forever."[2]

Our own experience confirms these truths. This world is full of suffering, evil, oppression, and death: infanticide, betrayal, rape, murder, genocide, and abuse. We do not have to look outside ourselves, however, to see these things. We have personally suffered misery and pain to one degree or another. We have caused others to suffer by our words and actions. And what is more, we are all going to die.

---

2. Committee on Christian Education of the Orthodox Presbyterian Church, *Confession*, 366. See also Romans 1–3.

Appreciating the need for a savior can be obscured, however, by God's goodness. We have good jobs, great marriages, healthy children, and nice homes. Who needs saving? When life is good, we should enjoy it and praise God for it. But the fact remains, we live in a sinful, fallen world, and sooner or later, our world will crash in on us. We lose our job, health, or family. Then all of a sudden, we are reminded that all is not well here. We are awakened to the fact that we need a savior. We need someone to deliver us from sin, misery, death, and Satan. We need a hero to make all wrongs right and to turn winter into spring.

Thankfully, God, in his goodness and incomparable love, has promised to save us from sin and death. He did so right after the fall, when he said to Adam and Eve, in Genesis 3:15, "I will put enmity between you [the devil] and the woman, and between your offspring and her offspring; he shall bruise your head, and you shall bruise his heel." In this verse, God promises that a descendent of Eve will one day come and destroy the devil: "he shall bruise your head."

The Battle between Good and Evil

Undoubtedly, Satan wasn't too pleased when he heard about God's promise to send someone to crush him and take away his newly acquired minions. His displeasure, though, was translated into action. He decided to fight back. The battle lines were thus drawn, and the war over humanity began in earnest between God and Satan.

Throughout the period leading up to the fulfillment of God's promise, if we would have pulled back the curtain to peer into what was going on behind the scenes, we would have seen the devil doing his best to eradicate the seed of the woman. He began with the ungodly Cain murdering his righteous brother Abel. Yet, the hope carried on in Eve's third son, Seth. Satan changed tactics and used marriage between the godly and the ungodly to wipe out the godly seed (Genesis 6). This approach nearly worked, as the newfound alliance diluted the true religion, causing humanity's wickedness to flourish, to the point where God decided to destroy humanity from the face of the earth. There was, however, one righteous man, Noah. God delivered him and his family from the flood, thereby keeping the hope of a future savior alive.

From the numerous peoples that came from Noah, God chose Abraham. The promised deliverer would be one of his descendents. A difficulty arose, however, in that Abraham's wife, Sarah, was unable to have any children (a consequence of the fall). As nothing is impossible with God, Sarah conceived and gave birth to the promised child, Isaac, in her old age. Isaac's wife, Rebekah, also had a hard time conceiving, yet God is faithful, and she eventually gave birth to twin boys, Esau and Jacob.

The promise carried on through Jacob. He had twelve sons, so the question of an heir was not an issue. Survival during the seven-year famine, however, was. To keep them and the promise alive, God used the wicked actions of ten sons to send one son, Joseph, to Egypt, so that he might be in a position to save them all from the severe famine. With Joseph being Pharaoh's right-hand man, Jacob and his family moved to Egypt, where after a long period of time, his family turned into a nation, containing as many people as the stars in the heavens.

At this juncture, Satan executed a violent assault on Israel in order to nullify God's promise. We learn in Exodus 1 that Pharaoh first enslaved the entire nation of Israel and then ordered the killing of all Hebrew male babies. Killing all the males would have effectively destroyed the nation, as the remaining girls would have been assimilated into the

Egyptian culture and people. The continuing line leading to the coming savior would have then been wiped out. God countered this attack through the Hebrew midwives who refused to carry out Pharaoh's orders, and by raising up Moses to lead his people out of Egypt.

While in the promised land, God chose Jesse's youngest son as the one through whom the savior would come. The Messiah would be a son of David. For a time, things went fairly smoothly, with just a few bumps in the road; but a tense moment occurred after the death of Ahaziah, the seventh king after David. Upon his death, Ahaziah's mother, Athaliah, killed all the royal heirs—that is, all the sons of David. She murdered all of them, except one. Unbeknownst to her, little Joash was rescued from among the king's sons who were being put to death. Satan was again frustrated after another close call. But though he lost another battle, he was far from giving up the war.

During the reign of Ahaz, Syria and Israel combined forces to blot out the house of David and set up their own king in Jerusalem (Isaiah 7). God promised to Ahaz that their attempt would fail: "It shall not stand, and it shall not come to pass" (Isa 7:7). To confirm his promise, God gave a sign: "Behold, the virgin shall conceive and bear a son, and shall call his name Immanuel" (Isa 7:14).

Further attempts were made by Satan to wipe out the line of the promised one: the exile due to the people's apostasy, the mixed marriages of the Jews who remained in Jerusalem, and the decree to exterminate the Jews during the time of Esther. All of them were unsuccessful, which set up a climactic battle, wherein Satan launched another violent assault to destroy the one who was supposed to destroy him. We will turn to this in a moment.

The point to be grasped is that there is a cosmic battle between good and evil. The Bible often describes it as the battle between two kingdoms: the kingdom of God and the kingdom of darkness. When we speak of the kingdom of God we do have to distinguish between God's kingdom in a redemptive sense and his kingdom in a providential sense. God is and always will be king and ruler over the world. As Nebuchadnezzar acknowledged, God's kingdom is an everlasting kingdom and he rules over all (Daniel 4). This is God's providential kingdom. But God's kingdom is also used in a redemptive sense, and it is this kingdom that is contrasted with the kingdom of Satan or darkness. This kingdom refers to God in time and history securing redemption and breaking the power of evil in this world.

In *The Lord of the Rings*, the hobbits live blissfully unaware of the great battle to save Middle Earth from the evil Sauron. Many people are like hobbits and do not understand or see the great battle waging between the kingdom of God and the kingdom of Satan, a battle over the allegiance of people's hearts and lives. But though they do not know it or admit it, the battle goes on. This is why believers must put on the whole armor of God daily: "For we do not wrestle against flesh and blood, but against the rulers, against the authorities, against the cosmic powers over this present darkness, against the spiritual forces of evil in the heavenly places" (Eph 6:12).

Jesus is the Promised Savior

The climactic battle between the two warring kingdoms began with the birth of Jesus, because he is the promised savior. With the appearance of his nemesis, Satan gathered his forces together for the showdown. Before we look at this part of the story, however, we want to demonstrate from the Gospels that Jesus, the son of Mary, is indeed God's promised savior.

A Portrait of Christ

The events surrounding Jesus' birth provided the first clues that he is the savior. Shortly after the birth of John the Baptist, the forerunner to Jesus, John's father, Zechariah, prophesied, saying in reference to Jesus that God had "raised up a horn of salvation for us in the house of his servant David, as he spoke by the mouth of his holy prophet from of old, that we should be saved from our enemies and from the hand of all who hate us" (Luke 1:69–71).

When an angel appeared to Mary to tell her that she would conceive and have a son, he said to her, "You shall call his name Jesus. He will be great and will be called the Son of the Most High. And the Lord God will give to him the throne of his father David, and he will reign over the house of Jacob forever, and of his kingdom there will be no end" (Luke 1:31–33).

Later on, as Joseph was thinking about quietly divorcing Mary because she had become pregnant, an angel appeared to him and said, "Joseph, son of David, do not fear to take Mary as your wife, for that which is conceived in her is from the Holy Spirit. She will bear a son and you shall call his name Jesus, for he will save his people from their sins" (Matt 1:20–21).

After his birth, Mary and Joseph took Jesus to the temple in Jerusalem. While there, Simeon took the child into his arms and blessed God, saying, "My eyes have seen your salvation that you have prepared in the presence of all peoples" (Luke 2:30–31).

Jesus' public ministry provided further clues that he is the savior. Right from the beginning of his ministry, Jesus proclaimed openly and with authority that "the kingdom of God is at hand" (Mark 1:15). In other words, it was time for the messianic kingdom of God to be established. The long-awaited kingdom was coming, because the long-awaited savior and king had come. It was time to dethrone Satan

The Promised Christ

and take away his power over people. It was time to see Satan fall like lightning from heaven (Luke 10:18).

Jesus' message of the nearness of the kingdom was confirmed by his casting out demons. In Mark 1:23–26, Jesus confronted a man possessed by an unclean spirit. Most of, if not all, the people witnessing this confrontation did not know who Jesus was or that he was the promised Messiah. The unclean spirit, however, knew exactly who Jesus was: "I know who you are—the Holy One of God" (Mark 1:24). He also knew what Jesus had come to do—that is, to redeem his people and conquer the reign of evil in the world. This is why the unclean spirit was defensive and said, "What have you to do with us, Jesus of Nazareth? Have you come to destroy us?" The demon recognized the nearness of the kingdom of God and was frightened. Jesus responded to the demon by commanding him to come out of the man. In so doing, Jesus demonstrated his power and authority over the kingdom of evil. He did this time and time again (Mark 1:32–34, 39). In fact, the abundance of unclean spirits during Jesus' time on earth was undoubtedly a result of his presence. The climactic battle between God and Satan had arrived.

Jesus' many miracles of healing also confirmed that he is the promised savior. Throughout the Gospels, we see Jesus healing the sick, making the blind see, cleansing lepers, and so forth. When John the Baptist was in prison, he began to wonder if Jesus was really the Messiah. So he sent his disciples to ask Jesus if he really was the one. Jesus responded, "Go and tell John what you hear and see: the blind receive their sight and the lame walk, lepers are cleansed and the deaf hear, and the dead are raised up, and the poor have good news preached to them" (Matt 11:4–5). Jesus was saying that he was indeed the Messiah, because he was doing the things that the Old Testament prophets said the Messiah would do (Isaiah 35; Luke 8:14–17).

Jesus' healing power highlighted the fact that he saves from sin and all of its consequences. To the paralytic man who wanted healing, Jesus said, "Son, your sins are forgiven" (Mark 2:5). Some of the scribes and Pharisees wondered what right Jesus had to forgive sins. And so Jesus said to them, "Which is easier, to say to the paralytic, 'Your sins are forgiven,' or to say, 'Rise, take up your bed and walk'?" (Mark 2:9). Jesus' miracles of healing demonstrated that he has power over the cause of sickness—namely, sin. In other words, he is the promised savior of sinners (and thus has the right to forgive sins), because he is able to save people from the consequences of sin: misery, sickness, and death.

Jesus' other miracles provided further evidence that he is the promised savior. After showing Nathanael his ability to know things that no ordinary person could know, Nathanael cried out, "Rabbi, you are the Son of God! You are the King of Israel!" (John 1:49). Upon his feeding the five thousand with five loaves of bread and two fish, the people said, "This is indeed the Prophet who is to come into the world!" (John 6:14). Although the people misunderstood Jesus' mission, they were right that Jesus is indeed the promised savior. And so his birth set the stage for the climactic battle between God and Satan.

The Climactic Battle

After Jesus was born in Bethlehem, wise men from the East went to Jerusalem looking for the one who had been born king of the Jews so that they might worship him. Upon learning from the chief priests and the scribes where the Christ was to be born, Herod told the wise men to go look in the little town of Bethlehem. He also directed them

The Promised Christ

to bring back news of his exact whereabouts. Ostensibly, Herod wanted to know where Jesus was living so that he, too, might worship him. But in reality, he felt threatened by this newborn king. So to protect his dynasty, Herod decided to kill the child.

Satan was, of course, working behind the scenes for his own purposes—namely, to kill the seed of the woman. After countless failed attempts, he could now taste victory. With the help of the Hebrew Scriptures and the bright star, the wise men found Jesus. Having worshipped him and given him gifts, they were ready to return to Jerusalem to tell Herod, who would not waste any time in killing the young king. The war would soon be over and he, Satan, would emerge triumphant.

God, however, is not one to be defeated. He warned the wise men in a dream to avoid Herod. So they returned to their own country by another way (Matt 2:12). God also warned Joseph in a dream to take Jesus and Mary and flee to Egypt for a time, because Herod was seeking to destroy Jesus. This Joseph did (Matt 2:14). And just in time, too! Because Herod became furious that the wise men did not return to him, and decided to put to death all the male children who were two years old and under in Bethlehem and all its districts (Matt 2:16). The Apostle John graphically depicts this scene and Satan's involvement in Revelation 12:3–5:

> And another sign appeared in heaven: behold, a great red dragon, with seven heads and ten horns, and on his heads seven diadems. His tail swept down a third of the stars of heaven and cast them to the earth. And the dragon stood before the woman who was about to give birth, so that when she bore her child he might devour it. She gave birth to a male child, one who is to

> rule all the nations with a rod of iron, but her
> child was caught up to God and to his throne.

Still, all was not lost for Satan. Although he had failed to keep the seed of the woman from coming into the world, there was still the opportunity to do to Jesus what he had done to Adam. Adam had led humankind into the kingdom of darkness. Jesus had come to lead us out. But if Satan could get Jesus to remain in his domain, then all would be well. And this is what he tried to do when he tempted Jesus in the wilderness.

Satan tempted Jesus, who was desperately hungry, to use his divine power to save himself by turning stones into bread. Although not a sin in and of itself, it would have been for Jesus, because it would have disqualified him from being our human mediator and savior. Appealing to Scripture, or rather twisting the meaning of Scripture, Satan urged Jesus to test God. Knowing that Jesus had come to take away his kingdom, Satan freely offered it to him, if only he will bow down and worship. Unlike Adam, Jesus resisted the devil at every turn, remaining faithful to his Father in heaven.

Destroying the devil, however, would require more work than simply resisting temptation. Jesus was going to have to go on the offensive and conquer Satan's stranglehold over us. In Matthew 12:28–29, Jesus interpreted his exorcisms with these words: "But if it is by the Spirit of God that I cast out demons, then the kingdom of God has come upon you. Or how can someone enter a strong man's house and plunder his goods, unless he first binds the strong man? Then indeed he may plunder his house." Jesus was going to bind Satan (the strong man) and plunder his house (lead us out of Satan's kingdom and into his own kingdom).

How Jesus did this exactly is nothing short of extraordinary. The devil was still desperate to eliminate Jesus. He enlisted Judas, unbelieving Jews, and Romans to execute

The Promised Christ

Jesus. In so doing, he undoubtedly thought he will win. But just the opposite happened—Jesus willingly laid down his life in order to crush and destroy Satan. By suffering and dying, Jesus administered the fatal blow and sets us free! As he said, "Now is the judgment of this world; now will the ruler of this world be cast out. And I, when I am lifted up from the earth, will draw all people to myself" (John 12:31–32; see also Col 2:13–15).

According to Revelation 20:3, Satan is now bound "so that he might not deceive the nations any longer." No more will Satan be allowed to entice us into sin, seduce us into error, and keep us under his influence. For he has been cast out as ruler and prince of this world. The seed of the woman has crushed the serpent's head. The works of the devil have been destroyed. Consequently, all authority and power now belong to the Lord Jesus Christ. This is why the good news of the gospel can go out into the world to tremendous success. Indeed, Paul was sent to preach the gospel to the Gentiles "to open their eyes, so that they may turn from darkness to light and from the power of Satan to God" (Acts 26:18). Hence, all who believe and receive the gospel are rescued "from the domain of darkness" and brought into "the kingdom of God's beloved Son" (Col 1:13).

Who is Jesus? Part of our answer needs to be that Jesus is the promised savior. He is the one that God has sent to conquer Satan, sin, and death. So if you want to be set free from Satan, sin, and death, then go to Jesus. If you want to serve God and receive eternal life, then follow Jesus. For he and he alone is the long-awaited Redeemer King.

2

The Divine-Human Savior

JESUS IS THE PROMISED savior. But who is he exactly? Who is this person that is able to deliver us from our enemies? Notice I did not ask, who would *like* to be our savior? Nor, who *thinks* he is our savior? I asked, who is *able* to be our savior? I may look at my sick child and desperately want to heal him, but be powerless to do so. I may look at my sick child and think I that I can heal him, but again be powerless to do so. So who is able to save us from our true enemies, including death itself, and bring us to the one true living God?

There is only one correct answer to this question, and that is Jesus, the God-man. Our savior must be both fully God and fully human in order to save us. And indeed, Jesus is just that: God incarnate.

The Humanity of Jesus

The Gospels make it painfully obvious that Jesus is a normal human being. He is fully and completely human, with a body, soul, mind, emotions, and so forth. His birth and

The Divine-Human Savior

subsequent development into an adult male provide the evidence.

When the angel Gabriel came to Mary, he told her that she was going to conceive in her womb and bear a son, a descendent of David (Luke 1:31–32, 35). Shortly thereafter, Mary became pregnant and went to visit Elizabeth. Elizabeth greeted Mary by saying that the child she was carrying was blessed (Luke 1:42). Nine months later, Joseph and Mary, "who was with child," were in Bethlehem, and "while they were there, the time came for her to give birth. And she gave birth to her firstborn son" (Luke 2:5–7). So like any normal human being, Jesus was conceived in his mother's womb, and nine months later, he was born.

Eight days after his birth, he was circumcised, like every other Jewish boy. When it was time, Mary and Joseph went to the temple to present the infant Jesus as a firstborn son to the Lord, according to the law of Moses. They then, along with their son, returned to Galilee, to the town of Nazareth. Luke writes that "the child grew and became strong, filled with wisdom" (Luke 2:40).

Several years later, when Jesus was still a boy, Mary and Joseph returned again to Jerusalem. While there, the boy Jesus went to the temple and sat among the teachers, listening to them and asking questions (Luke 2:46). Eventually, Jesus returned to his hometown with his parents, and Luke records that he "increased in wisdom and in stature and in favor with God and man" (Luke 2:52).

Like other children, Jesus had to obey his parents, go to school, and develop physically, mentally, and intellectually. He experienced the regular stages of human development: infant, boy, teenager, and adult.

Rich Mullins has a song that nicely captures the humanity of Jesus, particularly in his youth, entitled "Boy

A Portrait of Christ

Like Me/Man Like You."[1] In this song, Mullins talks about how Jesus was a boy and grew up just like him. He wonders what kind of games Jesus played, how Jesus reacted when he scraped his knee, and if the girls ever giggled when he walked past. It is a good song to remind us that Jesus is just like us.

In fact, Jesus is so like us that those who grew up with him had a hard time believing that he was someone special. After Jesus had begun his public ministry, Mark tells us that when he visited his hometown of Nazareth, the people he grew up with took offense at him. They said among themselves, "Where did this man get these things? What is the wisdom given to him? How are such mighty works done by his hands? Is not this the carpenter, the son of Mary and brother of James and Joses and Judas and Simon? And are not his sisters here with us?" (Mark 6:2–3; see also John 6:41–42 and John 8:57).

That Jesus is fully and completely human is explicitly stated or implied throughout the Gospels. Physically, he was exhausted, hungry, and thirsty (John 4:6; Matt 4:2; John 19:28). He rested, slept, and ate (Mark 6:31; 4:38; 2:15–16). He was whipped and beaten (John 19:1–3). Eventually, he was crucified and died (John 19:16–30). Emotionally, he rejoiced, celebrated, grieved, wept, marveled, recoiled at suffering, and became angry (Luke 10:21; John 2:1–12; Mark 3:5; John 11:35; Matt 8:10; Mark 14:32–36; 3:5). Relationally, he had family and friends whom he dearly loved, such as Lazarus, Mary, and Martha (Mark 3:31; John 11:5). Spiritually, he prayed, was tempted, was under the law, learned obedience, submitted to the will of God, attended synagogue, and studied the Scriptures (Matt 14:23; 4:1–16; Gal 4:4; Heb 5:8; Mark 14:36; Luke 4:44; 2:41–52).

1. Mullins, *The World as Best as I Remember It*, Reunion, 1991, compact disc.

The Divine-Human Savior

Intellectually, he grew in knowledge and wisdom (Luke 2:52; Mark 5:30; 9:21; 11:13). Inwardly, Jesus was troubled in his soul, had desires, and gave up his spirit when he died (John 12:27; 13:21; 17:24; 19:30).

Jesus is fully and completely human in mind, body, soul, spirit, and heart. He is not merely human, because he is also divine, as we will eventually see. But the fact that he is God does not diminish or change his humanity. Jesus is not a deified human or superman. Moreover, he is not part human. It is not as if his body is human but his soul is divine. The Son of God did not come down from heaven and possess a human body like an unclean spirit can possess a person. John 1:14 says that the Word became flesh. He became a human being. He is therefore a normal human being in every way, except of course, without sin.

The rest of the New Testament likewise stresses the humanity of Jesus. Paul often refers to Jesus as a man. Noting that sin and death came into the world through one man (Adam), Paul says that the free gift of righteousness came through "that one man Jesus Christ" (Rom 5:15). In 1 Timothy 2:5, Paul says that "there is one God and there is one mediator between God and men, the man Christ Jesus." Elsewhere, Paul notes that Jesus was born of a woman (Gal 4:4), was a descendent of Abraham and David (Gal 3:16; Rom 1:3), was a Jew by birth (Rom 9:5), and is the last Adam (1 Cor 15:45).

The author of Hebrews says that Jesus partook of flesh and blood and "had to be made like his brothers in every respect" (Heb 2:14, 17). He also notes that Jesus was a descendent of Judah (Heb 7:14). John, in his first epistle, mentions how he heard, saw, and touched with his own hands the Lord of glory (1 John 1:1–4), and that Jesus Christ has come in the flesh (1 John 4:2–3).

A Portrait of Christ

The Importance of the Humanity of Jesus

Why all this stress on the humanity of Christ? Is it really that necessary? Do I really need to believe that Jesus is a man to be saved? Was it really necessary that the Son of God become flesh in order to save us? The answer is an emphatic yes! In fact, the humanity of Christ is at the very heart of the gospel. To deny the full humanity of Christ, John says, is to deny the faith and imbibe the spirit of the antichrist (1 John 4:2–3).

Why is this so? Why is the humanity of Christ so important? First of all, there is no salvation without a human savior. The very reason the Son of God became a man was so that he might save us. Paul says that "God sent forth his Son, born of woman, born under the law, to redeem those who were under the law" (Gal 4:4–5). The author of Hebrews says that since the creatures to be saved were humans ("flesh and blood"), the Son of God shared in their humanity, so that through death he might destroy the devil. The author of Hebrews goes on to say that Jesus did not come to help angels but the offspring of Abraham. "Therefore he had to be made like his brothers in every respect . . . to make propitiation for the sins of the people" (Heb 2:14–17).

It was man who had sinned and it was man who had to die. Our savior, therefore, had to be a man in order to take our place, pay the penalty for our sins (death), and so redeem us from sin. To redeem angels, the savior would have had to become an angel. But the Father did not send his Son to save angels. Just as by one man (Adam) sin and death entered the world, so it is by one man (the last Adam) that there is now life and righteousness.

Another reason our savior had to become a man was in order to fulfill prophecy. God had promised that the seed of the woman would come to crush the head of

The Divine-Human Savior

the serpent. Furthermore, by becoming a man—by living, obeying, suffering, and dying as a man—Jesus is able to be a sympathetic savior. He knows experientially what it is to be a human. He knows perfectly how to help. Hence, with confidence, boldness, and assurance we can run to Jesus for mercy and grace.

The fundamental point is this: our savior needs to be fully human if we are going to be saved. This is why when people started denying the full humanity of our Lord, the early church fathers condemned them as heretics. For this point is no minor theological quibble. It is a fundamental article of the faith. Our salvation depends upon it. Christ had to become human in every way (body and soul) in order to save us in every way. John of Damascus said, "For the whole Christ assumed the whole me that he might grant salvation to the whole me, for what is unassumable is incurable."[2]

If the Son of God had not been conceived by the Holy Spirit in the womb of Mary and born of her, then we would still be in our sins and without any hope. But the good news of great joy that the angels said to the shepherds on the very first Christmas is this: "For unto you is born this day in the city of David a Savior, who is Christ the Lord. And this will be a sign for you: you will find a baby wrapped in swaddling cloths and lying in a manger" (Luke 2:11–12).

The Divinity of Jesus

One cannot read the Gospels, or indeed the rest of the New Testament, and not come to the conclusion that Jesus is God. As B. B. Warfield once said, "The deity of Christ is in

---

2. Quoted by Bavinck, *Reformed Dogmatics*, 3:297.

A Portrait of Christ

solution in every page of the New Testament."[3] Consider first of all the events surrounding Jesus' birth. They were unique to say the least. The angel Gabriel told Mary that she was going to conceive and bear a son, whom she was to call Jesus. This she was going to do even though she was a virgin, because "the Holy Spirit will come upon [her], and the power of the Most High will overshadow [her]" (Luke 1:35). After Jesus was born, an angel appeared to shepherds out in a field to announce his birth, saying, "For unto you is born this day in the city of David a Savior, who is Christ the Lord" (Luke 2:11). Then a great multitude of angels appeared and praised God and rejoiced over the birth of Jesus (Luke 2:13).

Clearly then, the manner of Jesus' conception and the presence of angels at his birth indicate that he is someone special. But the fact that the angel called him "the Lord" teaches us just how special he is. The word "Lord" is most commonly used in the Greek translation of the Old Testament to translate "Yahweh," the name of God. It is in this sense that the word "Lord" is being used.[4] So the angel was saying to the shepherds that in the city of David , a savior is born who is Christ (i.e., the Messiah), and this Christ is God himself!

Consider second the divine attributes that Jesus displayed during the course of his public ministry. In the Gospels, we see that Jesus knew things a mere man could not have known. Even though he was far away, he knew that Nathanael was under a fig tree. Such knowledge led Nathanael to proclaim, "Rabbi, you are the Son of God! You are the King of Israel!" (John 1:47–49). Similarly, Jesus knew the life history of the Samaritan woman (John 4), what people were thinking (Mark 2:8; Matt 9:4), when

3. Warfield, "Deity," 1:153.

4. See Grudem, *Systematic Theology*, 544.

The Divine-Human Savior

Lazarus died (John 11:11, 14), those among his followers who did not truly believe, and even the one who would betray him (John 6:64).

Now it could be argued that Jesus was told all of these things by God, much like a prophet. But the Gospels do not say that he was told these things. In fact, Scripture says that his knowledge was not limited to a few scattered facts, like it would have been with a prophet. John says that he knows the hearts of all people (John 2:24–25) and that he knows all things (John 16:30; 21:17). Thus, the Gospels depict Jesus as omniscient, which is a divine attribute.

The many miracles that Jesus performed, such as walking on water and calming the storm at sea with a word, demonstrate his divine power. What is striking about many of Jesus' miracles is that he did them by his own power and on his own authority. He didn't pray to God for help to do the miracle, he simply said the word and it was done.

This was most evident in Jesus' calming the storm at sea. With a word, he rebuked the wind and the waves, and immediately they were still. Psalm 65:7 says that God is the one who stills the roaring of the seas and the roaring of the waves (see also Ps 107:29). God the Creator has control over his creation. Yet, here was Jesus calming the wind and waves with a word. No wonder his disciples became more afraid of Jesus than they were of the storm and said, "Who then is this, that even the wind and sea obey him?" (Mark 4:41). This is why his mighty miracles are said to manifest his glory (John 2:11). By contrast, Elijah's miracles did not manifest his glory, but God's glory!

Consider third that Jesus claimed for himself various divine prerogatives. He declared to have the right to forgive people of their sins (Mark 2:10); he referred to the angels as "his angels" (Matt 13:41; 16:27; 24:31); he asserted that he had all authority and power (Matt 11:25–27; 28); he taught with self-attesting authority (Matt 5:22); he said that he would judge all men and angels (Matt 25:31–31; John 5:22); and he declared that people must honor him even as they honor the Father, and if they do not honor him, then they are not honoring the Father (John 5:23).

Consider fourth that the Gospels assert Jesus' preexistence. Numerous times, John writes in his Gospel that Jesus came down from heaven. To come down from heaven implies that he existed before he was conceived. John the Baptist was born before Jesus, and yet he testified that Jesus was far greater than him because Jesus was before him (John 1:15). Even though Abraham walked the earth hundreds of years before he was born, Jesus says in John 8:55 that he knew Abraham. And then in verse 58 he says, "Truly, truly, I say to you, before Abraham was, I am." In so doing, Jesus claimed the name of God for himself, a claim that did not go unnoticed by the scribes and Pharisees (John 5:18; 19:7).

That Jesus is God is clear from what we have seen thus far, but it all comes together and is made quite explicit in John 1. In the opening verses of his Gospel, John refers to Jesus as "the Word." We will see the reasons for this in a moment, but notice for now that John implicitly says that Jesus is God by placing him at creation and by attributing to him the work of creation: "In the beginning was the Word ... He was in the beginning with God. All things were made through him, and without him was not any thing made that was made" (John 1:1–3).

John also explicitly says that Jesus is God: "and the Word was God" (John 1:1). Furthermore, he points out that though Jesus is God, he is also distinct from God. Verse 1: "and the Word was with God"; and verse 18: "at the Father's side." This indicates that Jesus is a separate or distinct person from God the Father. Here we see in part what amounts to the doctrine of the Trinity. There is one God and this one

The Divine-Human Savior

God exists in three persons, the Father, the Son, and the Spirit. Jesus is God the Son. In verse 14, John identifies the Word with the Son.

Thus, God the Son is the one who became a human being. John 1:14: "and the Word became flesh and dwelt among us." Literally, John says, "tabernacled" among us. Instead of God dwelling in a tent or tabernacle, he now dwells in human form. God, therefore, relates and dwells with us in the most personal and intimate way possible—that is, by becoming one of us.

Consequently, John says that when he and his disciples saw Jesus, they saw "his glory, glory as of the only Son from the Father, full of grace and truth" (John 1:14). John seems to be alluding to Moses seeing the glory of God in Exodus 33 and to the glory of God that filled the tabernacle in Exodus 40. The glory of God is no longer revealed in a pillar of cloud, but in Jesus Christ, our Lord.

Since Jesus is God, John is able to say that Jesus has made known the invisible God (John 1:18). The phrase "made him known" is variously translated as "explained him" (NASB) and "declared him" (NKJV). We derive the word "exegesis" from this Greek word. Elsewhere in the New Testament it means "to tell a narrative" or "to narrate." So John is saying that Jesus reveals God.

This is why John calls Jesus "the Word." In the Old Testament, the "word" of the Lord is God's powerful self-expression in creation, revelation, and salvation. It was by the "word" that God created, revealed himself through his prophets, and saved his people. Therefore, Jesus, who is God's ultimate manifestation or revelation, is appropriately called the "Word." In this light, Jesus' response to Philip's request to show them the Father makes perfect sense: "Whoever has seen me has seen the Father" (John 14:9; see also John 20:28).

The Importance of the Divinity of Jesus

The Gospels, then, proclaim that the promised savior is God himself. But why did the savior have to be divine? Was it really necessary for him to be God? Did it really take God himself to come down from heaven to save his people?

Well, the Old Testament indicates that the one true savior is God. Consider the following passages: "The LORD is my rock and my fortress and my deliverer, my God, my rock, in whom I take refuge, my shield, and the horn of my salvation, my stronghold. I call upon the LORD, who is worthy to be praised, and I am saved from my enemies" (Ps 18:2–3); "Salvation belongs to the LORD" (Ps 3:8); "I, I am the LORD, and besides me there is no savior" (Isa 43:11); "But I am the LORD your God from the land of Egypt; you know no God but me, and besides me there is no savior" (Hos 13:4); "Salvation belongs to the LORD!" (Jonah 2:9).

So in order to be true to Scripture, the savior had to be God. But he also had to be God in order to accomplish salvation. The wages of sin is death, eternal death. A mere human would need all eternity to fully satisfy the punishment for sin. The eternal God, however, is able to pay an eternal debt in a moment. Therefore, unless God comes to save us, we are without hope. When Jesus was praying in the garden of Gethsemane, he asked the Father if there was another way. If there had been another way, the Father would have granted his Son's wish. But there wasn't. We needed a divine savior.[5]

---

5. Committee on Christian Education of the Orthodox Presbyterian Church, *Confession*, 181–82.

The Divine-Human Savior

Jesus is the God-Man

Who is Jesus, our promised deliverer? We have seen that he is fully human in every respect and that he is also fully divine in every respect. The question is how we put these two plain truths together. And it is precisely here that we begin to delve into the mystery of the incarnation. Yet, it is important that we do not put them together incorrectly. It is the Son of God who came down from heaven and took on humanity. He, therefore, now has a divine nature and a human nature.

Jesus is not two persons, a divine person and a human person. He has a human will and consciousness, and a divine will and consciousness. Nevertheless, he is not two persons. He didn't inhabit or take over another human person. He took on an impersonal human nature. So Jesus doesn't have a split personality. He doesn't talk to himself or within himself. The human Jesus doesn't talk to the divine Jesus, because he is one person.

Jesus does not have one nature that is only partly human and partly divine. The divine nature and human nature are not mixed together to form a hybrid nature, in which Jesus' human nature takes on divine characteristics, or vice versa. Jesus' human body, for example, can only be in one place at one time. Jesus is one person, the Son of God, with two natures: divine and human.

This means that when Jesus was an infant in his mother's arms, he was at the same time upholding the universe by the word of his power (Heb 1:3). He who was exhausted from a long day's work and fast asleep on the boat was also the Sovereign Ruler of the universe. He was "tired yet omnipotent!"[6] He who was dying on the cross was

---

6. Grudem, *Systematic Theology*, 559.

also sustaining the lives of those who had crucified him. He knows all things and yet does not know some things.

Jesus is one person with two distinct natures. This also means that what he does by one nature is ascribed to the person. In other words, what is true of either nature is true of the person. Hence, the Bible can speak of God doing certain things that technically only a human can do, like die, because it was the Son of God as the God-man who did these things. Acts 20:28 says that God obtained the church with his own blood. God cannot die, obviously. But Jesus, the Son of God, died, and by his death saved us from eternal death. By means of his humanity, he was able to take our place and suffer and die for us, while by his divinity he was able to satisfy an eternal debt.

Jesus, the God-man, is the one and only savior. Therefore, whoever believes in Jesus will not perish but have everlasting life. And whoever does not believe in Jesus is condemned already, because he has not believed in the name of the only Son of God (John 3:16–18).

3

The Compassionate Christ

God is not a physical being. He is spirit (John 4:24) and therefore he is invisible (1 Tim 1:17). For this reason, the Bible says in numerous places that God cannot be seen and that no one has seen Him (1 Tim 6:16; 1 John 4:12; John 1:18; 6:46). However, there is a sense in which we will be able to see God with our own eyes when we look into the face of Jesus Christ, because he is both God and man. God the Son, having been sent by God the Father, came down from heaven and was conceived in the womb of Mary by the power of God the Spirit. The Son, therefore, took on humanity and became a man. He became flesh and dwelt among us.

The Son did not lay aside any of his divine attributes or stop being God in order to become a man. That would have been impossible, because God cannot stop being God. Rather, God became a human. An addition took place in the incarnation, not a subtraction. God, remaining God, became a man. This is why we affirm in our creeds and confessions that Jesus is both God and man. He is one person (God the Son) with two natures (divine and human).

A Portrait of Christ

Since Jesus is God the Son, and thus truly and completely God, Paul can say that "in him the whole fullness of deity dwells bodily" (Col 2:9; see also 1:19), and that he is "the image of the invisible God" (Col 1:15). The word "image" means an exact visible representation. Hebrews 1:3 says that Jesus is the exact imprint of the nature of God. Jesus perfectly reveals to us the very nature and character of God. In Jesus, the invisible becomes visible. Hence, Jesus can say to Phillip that in seeing him, he sees the Father (John 14:9). And why John can say that Jesus reveals the Father (John 1:18).

So when we look at Jesus, we are looking at God. Now of course, if we were to look at Jesus, we would see his human body; but the person we would see, meet, and know would be none other than God himself. This is one of the marvelous benefits of the incarnation. God reveals himself to us in the most concrete and accommodating fashion. To see and know the man Christ Jesus is to see and know God himself!

Seen in this light, the Gospels become priceless. While they are not a typical biography, they do provide an account of Jesus' life here on earth, from which we can discover much about him. We learn what he is like, what he did, what he said, how he lived his life, and so forth. By means of such information, we grow in our knowledge of God. For the life of Christ is a window in heaven's door.

Thus, as we turn our attention from who Jesus is to what he is like, we need to keep in mind that in so doing, we will grow in our appreciation of who God is. We also need to understand that Jesus' life is something we are to imitate. It is true that we are not to imitate him in everything, because he is Christ the Lord. Nevertheless, as the perfect man, his life is a pattern we are to follow (1 Cor 11:1; 1 Pet 2:21). Revelation and imitation flow from the incarnation.

The Compassionate Christ

We are going to begin our study of Jesus' character by looking at the related attributes of love, compassion, mercy, and kindness. Love for people in sin, misery, and death expresses itself internally in the emotions of compassion or pity and externally in the works of compassion or mercy. There would be no need for these things in an unfallen world. But in a fallen world, where suffering is a way of life, love works itself out in compassion, pity, and mercy.

This is precisely what we see in the life of Jesus, who came down from heaven and dwelled among us in this sin-cursed world. In fact, Jesus' whole life was so marked by deeds of mercy that Peter could summarize his public life with these words: "He went about doing good" (Acts 10:38).

How do you feel or respond when you see a fellow human being suffering in one way or another? How do you react when you see someone dying of cancer, a child wasting away because of malnutrition, a man suffering from severe depression, a woman suffering from a broken heart, or a friend who is spiritually blind and destitute?

You could be cold or indifferent: an "I don't care" or "I'm glad it is you and not me" attitude. You could be cruel and rub their noses in their own pain. Or you could be moved with pity and compassion to help them. It is this third response that we see time and time again in the life of Christ.

Jesus' Compassion toward the Physically Oppressed

Early on in his public ministry, a leper went to Jesus on his knees, begging the Lord to make him clean (Mark 1:40–45). Since there was no cure for leprosy, lepers were forced to live apart from society, and to die in isolation from friends and family. The life of a leper was truly sad. It is not surprising, then, to find a leper coming to Jesus and begging for his help. Jesus was deeply affected by his plight and his plea. Mark writes that he was "moved with pity" and touched him, saying, "be clean."

Jairus, a synagogue ruler, came to Jesus one day because his daughter was on her death bed. He implored Jesus to come to his home and lay his hands on her to save her life. The Lord followed Jairus to his house, but on the way the report came that the little girl had died. Overhearing this, and undoubtedly realizing the pain this would inflict upon Jairus, Jesus quickly said to him, "Do not fear, only believe" (Mark 5:36). Jesus then went to the girl and raised her from the dead.

Having left Jericho, Jesus was walking along the road, where two blind men were sitting by the roadside (Matt 20:29–34). When they heard that Jesus was passing by, they cried out, "Lord, have mercy on us, Son of David!" They continued crying out, despite people telling them to keep quiet. It is helpful to note that blind people, like lepers, did not have an easy life in ancient times. Many of them were forced to beg for a living. In fact, the two blind men were probably on the side of the road in order to beg for money. But when they heard that Jesus was coming, they cried out for help. Upon hearing them, Jesus stopped and asked them what they wanted him to do for them. They asked for their sight. Matthew 20:34 then says, "And Jesus in pity touched their eyes, and immediately they recovered their sight and followed him."

In Mark 8, Jesus noticed that the huge crowd that had been with him for three days to hear him teach were hungry but had nothing to eat. Jesus said to his disciples that he felt compassion for the crowd and did not want to send them away hungry because some might have fainted on the way to their homes.

The Compassionate Christ

Luke records a very moving account of Jesus' interaction with a widow at her only son's funeral procession (Luke 7:11–17). Here was a woman utterly heartbroken and perhaps overcome with worry about her future and how she would survive. When Jesus saw her, his heart swelled with compassion, and he gently said to her, "Do not weep." Then he walked over to the casket and raised the young man from the dead. Similarly, in John 11, Jesus was so moved with compassion and sympathy at the death of his dear friend, Lazarus, and the grief it caused his sisters, Mary and Martha, that he wept.

From this brief survey, we begin to understand that Jesus was grieved and pained to see people suffer from the physical and emotional consequences of sin. He felt compassion and pity from the depths of his being for those in need, in pain, and in grief. He didn't dismiss people's pain by saying that they got what they deserved. Nor did he help people in their distress with coldness, indifference, or simply because it was the right thing to do. Jesus sympathized, he was moved by pity and compassion. Our pain causes him pain. It was from this emotional response that he helped those in need.

It is important that we do not misinterpret or misapply these many passages of healing. Many years ago, when I was in seminary, a woman was explaining to me that she felt assured that her husband would be cured of his prostate cancer. The reason for her assurance was that in her morning devotions she had read about God telling Hezekiah that he would be healed from his fatal illness. She took that passage to mean that God was telling her that he would heal her husband.

While we may not read the Bible incorrectly, like this woman, we may begin wonder, in light of all of these passages of healing, why the Lord does not heal me or heal my loved one. After all, if the Lord is so compassionate, why doesn't he heal me? Does the fact that I am not healed, even though I have begged him in prayer many times, mean he doesn't care about me or that he feels no pity for me?

We need to understand that Jesus did not devote himself primarily to healing. He could have spent his whole time in healing the sick, raising the dead, and casting out demons. But he refrained, because he did not come to bring temporary relief to those in need. Rather, he came to bring eternal relief, healing that would usher in eternal life.

In Mark 1, after his fame grew quickly because of his healings, Jesus escaped the crowds by leaving town. When Simon found him, he said, "Everyone is looking for you." But Jesus did not return to the people, nor did he heal more of them. Rather, he said, "Let us go on to the next towns, that I may preach there also, for that is why I came out" (Mark 1:38).

Jesus came to preach the gospel. He came to save people from their sins and eternal death. He did not come primarily to heal the sick, cast out demons, and raise the dead for a few more years of life. These miracles, which the New Testament calls signs, pointed to the fact that Jesus had come to conquer the root cause of sickness, demon possession, and death—namely, sin and Satan. His miracles served to confirm and support his preaching that the kingdom of God was coming!

Nevertheless, Jesus did feel compassion for those suffering, and it moved him to temporarily heal people and raise them from the dead. This does teach us about Jesus' character, and indeed the character of God. The Old Testament is full of passages detailing and demonstrating the compassion, kindness, and love of God. Exodus 2:24 says that God heard the groaning of the people of Israel and acted to save them. Deuteronomy 30:3 says that God will

The Compassionate Christ

restore his people from exile, because of his compassion for them.

It is one thing to say that God is compassionate, and another to see his compassion in action in the Exodus. But it is still another to see the compassion of our God in the person of our Lord Jesus Christ. Upon witnessing our suffering, Jesus was moved with pity to the point of groaning and weeping.

The compassion of God as revealed in the person of Jesus is what we need to cling to when we go through trials and difficulties. While the Lord has his reasons for not always relieving our suffering, he is ever and always compassionate toward us. We truly do have a sympathetic high priest. He knows from a human point of view what it is like to see fellow human beings suffer and what it is like to suffer. He weeps when we weep. He hurts when we hurt. Hence, when we are hurting, we should run confidently to Jesus to receive mercy and grace (Heb 4:14–16).

But we do not only run to Jesus when we are physically or emotionally hurt. We can boldly run to Him when we are suffering spiritually, because he is also compassionate toward those who are spiritually destitute and those who are caught in the clutches of sin.

Jesus' Compassion toward the Spiritually Oppressed

In Mark 6, Jesus went ashore and saw a great crowd waiting for him. As he looked out upon the crowd, Mark tells us that "he had compassion on them, because they were like sheep without a shepherd. And he began to teach them many things" (Mark 6:34). There is perhaps nothing more detrimental for sheep than not having a shepherd. Sheep are absolutely helpless without a shepherd to guide them,

A Portrait of Christ

to protect them, and to lead them to grazing fields. Sheep without a shepherd will not survive very long. In Ezekiel 34, God accuses the shepherds of Israel of abandoning the people of Israel, because they fed themselves instead of the sheep. It was for this reason that the people standing before Jesus were like sheep with no shepherd. Not that they had no shepherds—they had the scribes and Pharisees—but these shepherds were terrible. And as a result, the people were confused and hungry, with no one to lead and feed them. Seeing the people in such a sad state deeply affected the Lord.

We also see Jesus' compassion for those hardened in unbelief. Near the end of his life, when he was approaching Jerusalem, Jesus wept because of the destruction that would befall her unrepentant inhabitants. B. B. Warfield describes the scene: "The sight of suffering drew tears from his eyes; obstinate unbelief convulsed him with uncontrollable grief . . . It hurt Jesus to hand over even hardened sinners to their doom."[1]

Jesus' tears over hardened and stubborn Jerusalem poignantly express divine compassion for the ungodly. Second Chronicles 36:15 says that the Lord continually sent warnings to his people, urging them to repent, because he had compassion on them. Isaiah calls upon the wicked to forsake his way and "return to the Lord, that he may have compassion on him, and to our God, for he will abundantly pardon" (Isa 55:7). Ezekiel declares that God has no pleasure in the death of the wicked, but rather desires that everyone should turn from his evil way and live (Ezek 18:23, 32; 33:11). Indeed, the Lord pled with Israel saying, "turn back, turn back from your evil ways, for why will you die, O house of Israel?" (Ezek 33:11). God is indeed a compassionate and merciful God.

---

1. Warfield, "Emotional Life," 44–45.

The Compassionate Christ

Although we may have fallen into grievous sin or fallen away, even for a long time, we can run confidently to Jesus, in repentance and faith, knowing that he will forgive us. He will rejoice over us and break out the fattened calf on our behalf (Luke 15:30). For he is the compassionate savior of sinners!

4

The Compassionate Christ, Part 2

THE NATURE, INTENSITY, AND expression of a person's love and compassion are directly related to the type of relationship that person has with the one he loves. For example, I am to love my enemy, my neighbor, and my wife. But the type of love and the way I love will vary quite drastically between the three. Obviously, the kind of love I have (or at least should have) for my neighbor will be different from the kind of love I have for my children. The type of relationship dictates the type of love that is to be shown. The most special human relationship is that between a husband and wife. Thus, the deepest, longest, widest, and most special love is the love a husband is to have for his wife, and vice versa. The Lord Jesus Christ loves and is compassionate to all persons, even to hardened, unrepentant sinners. Yet, it is also true that he loves the church, his bride, in a very special and saving way.

Jesus' Compassion and Love are Seen in His Caring for His People in the Midst of His Own Suffering

If we are in the midst of personal crisis or terrible suffering, it is hard enough to keep our own head above water, let alone worry about other people and help them survive their own troubles. Isn't it true that when we are hurting, sick, or in trouble, our selfishness rises to the top? In our suffering, we desire that others look after us, meet our needs, and cater to our every whim. In Jesus, however, we see just the opposite. In the midst of tremendous suffering, he was still concerned about the welfare of his disciples. Even while walking in the valley of the shadow of death, he took care of his troubled disciples.

The Son of God came down from heaven to take away the sins of the world. As a man, therefore, Jesus fully experienced (mentally, physically, spiritually) the horror this mission unleashed upon him. In bearing the penalty of sin, he truly was the man of sorrows. As his death approached, Jesus cried out, "Now is my soul troubled" (John 12:27).

Prior to his betrayal, trial, beating, and crucifixion, Jesus was greatly distressed and troubled. He even poured out his aching heart to his disciples, saying, "My soul is very sorrowful, even to death" (Mark 14:34). Jesus' affliction was so great that he was sinking under the weight of it. Luke tells us that his sweat became like great drops of blood falling down to the ground, and that an angel came to strengthen him (Luke 22:43–44). Our Lord was going through hell as he was approaching hell. It wasn't the mere prospect of physical death that caused Jesus to be in such agony, but it was because he was going to suffer at the hands of Satan, the one who has the power of death (Heb 2:14). He was going to experience the full extent of the wrath of God for sin and be forsaken by his Father in heaven.

A Portrait of Christ

No wonder, then, that Jesus naturally recoiled at the idea of having to drink the cup his Father had given him to drink (Luke 22:42). Yet, on the night of his betrayal, he was deeply concerned about his disciples. While their situation did not even compare to that of Jesus, the disciples were deeply troubled and their hearts were filled with a medley of emotions. Jesus was about to leave them, because he was going to die. He told them that one of them would betray him. He also told Peter that he would deny Jesus three times. In fact, all of them would desert him. In light of what they thought about themselves, Jesus, and the messianic mission, these things were simply too much for them. Consequently, they were profoundly confused and unsettled.

Jesus saw the worried look on their faces and gently said to them, "Let not your hearts be troubled" (John 14:1) and "Let not your hearts be troubled, neither let them be afraid" (John 14:27). Literally, Jesus said, "Stop being troubled in your heart." In other words, Jesus knew their hearts were disturbed and he lovingly commanded them to stop. He is like the parent who hates the fact that his child is "troubled" at the prospect of going to the doctor, and so seeks to comfort and reassure him.

Jesus, of course, didn't just tell them to stop being troubled. He explained to them why they should not be troubled. He told them to trust in him because he was going to prepare a place for them and will eventually bring them to where he is. In short, they were not to worry, because everything in the end will work out gloriously. But in the meantime, he will give them peace and send the Holy Spirit to abide in them and guide them. So even though Jesus was deeply distressed, his love for his disciples compelled him to be compassionate toward them in their time of need.

We see this same love and compassion in a most vivid manner directed toward two individuals: Peter and Mary,

The Compassionate Christ, Part 2

the mother of Jesus. In Luke 22:31, Jesus said to Peter, "Simon, Simon, behold, Satan demanded to have you, that he might sift you like wheat, but I have prayed for you that your faith may not fail. And when you have turned again, strengthen your brothers." Jesus is himself about to be handed over to Satan, and yet here he is praying for Peter.

People familiar with the Gospels know the story of Peter's denial of the Lord. But what some may not have noticed is that after the third denial and the crowing of the rooster, Luke says that the Lord turned and looked at Peter (Luke 22:61). Our Lord was thinking of Peter while he was on trial. Not wanting Peter to fall away or become hardened in sin, Jesus turned and looked at him. What kind of look do you think Jesus gave Peter? What did Peter see when he turned his eyes to Jesus? Jesus knew what it was like to be tempted. In fact, he was being tempted at that moment. Moreover, Jesus was aware that Satan was sifting Peter as wheat and trying to do to Peter what he had done to Judas. And so the Lord was praying for Peter. What kind of look then do you think he gave Peter? Surely, it was a look of love and concern, a look that would have pierced Peter's heart and broken it. For when Peter's eyes met the gaze of his Lord, he remembered what the Lord had said to him. And he went out and wept bitterly.

Jesus expressed the same compassion toward his mother. In Luke 2:35, Simeon told Mary that one day a sword would pierce through her soul because of her firstborn son. That day came when she stood by her son hanging on the shameful cross, watching him die. Despite his own grief and suffering, Jesus was sensitive to his mother's anguish, as he lovingly provided for his mother by having John become like a son to her (John 19:26–27).

A Portrait of Christ

Jesus' Love and Compassion for His People are Seen in His Prayers and Desires

In John 17:9, Jesus prayed, not for the world, but for those whom the Father had given to him. Here we see Jesus' special love for his people. He prayed in this instance only for his own, asking the Father to keep them from the evil one, to sanctify them in the truth, to unite them, and to bring them to where he is and see his glory.

This last request is particularly striking because it expresses our Lord's heartfelt desire. John 17:24 says, "Father, I desire that they also, whom you have given me, may be with me where I am, to see my glory that you have given me." Without a doubt, this request shows that Jesus loves his own with a heartfelt, tender love. This can be seen more clearly when we contrast what is said here with similar expressions.

In John 14:1–3, Jesus told his disciples not to let their hearts be troubled, because he was going away to prepare a place for them, and he will come back for them so that they might be where he is. Similarly, Jesus said to the suffering thief on the cross, "Truly, I say to you, today you will be with me in Paradise" (Luke 23:43). Now it is one thing for Christ to comfort us by saying that he will most definitely deliver us from all of our trouble and pain by taking us to himself. It is another, and much greater, thing for him to yearn for our presence.

Imagine for a moment that I have a nephew, known to be a troublemaker, who has just been orphaned and needs a place to stay. My wife asks me what I think we should do. I could respond in several ways. First, I could say something like this: "Even though he is a difficult child and I don't really want to look after him, I think we should have him come and live with us. It would be much better for him to stay in a Christian home than in a secular foster home."

Or second: "The right thing to do, regardless of whether or not we might find another good home, is that he needs to stay with us. We may not like it, but we promised to do it, and so we must love him and take care of him."

Finally: "I would love to have my nephew stay with us. That is my heart's desire and pleasure. I would be devastated if he did not come and live with us." It is the last response that best captures the spirit of Jesus' prayer in John 17:24. He does not ask for his own to be with him merely because that is what is best for them or simply because it is the right thing to do, but because that is his heart's aspiration. This is what he longs for! And so he asks his Father for it! Robert M. M'Cheyne's sermon on this passage contains this striking sentence: "In truth, Christ cannot [lack] you. You are His jewels—His crown. Heaven would be no heaven to Him, if you were not there." [1]

Amazingly, Jesus wants his people to be with him. For this reason, it is proper to view the death of Christians as the Father answering his Son's prayer. Benjamin Morgan Palmer once eloquently said:

> Now, one of the strongest instincts of the human soul is the longing to be with those whom you love. Ah, my brethren, need I tell that to you? How many wear the badges of mourning, and draw down those crape veils over your faces! Do you not know all about the wrench, when death comes and tears away from your embrace those who made the joy of life to you? In your thoughts of your dead, have you never experienced that strange hunger of the heart when you long to bring them back and fold them within

[1]. Bonar, *Memoir*, 470.

the embrace of your affection? As you kneel in your grief by the fresh-made grave, and your thoughts go down into the low and dark abode where they are sleeping, you could with your very fingers scrape away the earth which hides them from your sight, in this longing to hold fellowship with them again. Well, our divine Redeemer is our Elder Brother, bone of our bone and flesh of our flesh; and there in the heavens He feels the pulse of those human affections of which we are so distinctly conscious, and breaks out—I had almost said into the passionate cry, 'Father, I will that they also, whom thou hast given me, be with me where I am.' Let it comfort you when you are called upon to give up your dead, that, if it break your fellowship with them and subject you to this strange hunger of love, you give them up to Jesus, whom you love more than you love yourself, and who has the same longing for their presence and society above. When death comes, as His messenger, over the threshold of your home, and says to you, as he touches with his skeleton finger child or parent, or husband or wife, 'The Master hath need of them'—'loose them and let them go;' and lay the solace upon your heart that your Friend, who has redeemed both you and them, is longing for their society above. If they part from you, it is only that they may be folded within His arms and lay their aching heads upon His bosom forever.[2]

---

2. Palmer, *Sermons*, 1:395–6.

Jesus' Love and Compassion for His People are Seen in How He Loved His People

John 13:1 says that "Jesus knew that his hour had come to depart out of this world to the Father," and "having loved his own who were in the world, he loved them to the end." "To the end" may mean to the end of his life or it may mean "to the uttermost" or "to the full extent of his love." Even if the meaning is "to the end of his life," the idea of "to the uttermost" is still applicable because of the way in which Christ loved his people during the last days of his life. In John 15, Jesus says that there is no greater love than this: that someone lay down his life for his friends. This is exactly what Jesus did for his friends.

Jesus came to this earth and died on the cross out of love for his people. Yes, he laid down his life because of his love for the Father and his willingness to do the Father's will. Yet, he also went to the cross because he loved his people. Hence, he says in John 15:9 that as the Father has loved him so he has loved his own. Truly, there is no greater love than the love the Father has for the Son. Yet, that is precisely the kind of love the Son has for his church. Jesus has loved his bride to the uttermost.

One of Satan's chief tactics to destroy a believer is to get him to doubt God's love. He used this tactic in the garden and it worked. He persuaded Adam and Eve to believe that God was holding out on them and did not have their best interest in mind. If such a plan can work in a perfect world, you can be sure that it will work in a fallen, sin-cursed world, where our trials, difficulties, and hardships can be used by Satan to make us think that God does not truly love us. The puritan Thomas Manton wrote:

> [Satan] seeks to hide God's goodness, and to represent him as a God that delights in our

> destruction and damnation, rather than in our salvation; as if he were inexorable, and hardly entreated to do us good. And why? That we may stand aloof from God, and apprehend him as unlovely. Or if he cannot prevail so far, he tempts us to poor, unworthy, mean thoughts of his goodness and mercy.[3]

In the person of the Lord Jesus Christ we see the very embodiment of God's love for us. Jesus, who is God and man, is the Father's gift of love to us, but also the very expression and revelation of his love for us. Can there really be a greater expression and revelation of God's love for us than his Son? If Christ dearly loved his own and took care of his own while he was suffering here on earth, will he not do the same for us today, now that he is in glory with all authority and power?

While there may be many reasons in this sin-cursed world to doubt that God loves us, Jesus overrules them all. His very presence among us, his compassionate love, and ultimately his death prove that God loves us with an incomparable love and that he truly works in all things for the good of those who love him and who have been called according to his purpose (Rom 8:28).

---

3. Manton, "Sermon XVI," 2:342.

5

Christ the Friend

IN THIS FALLEN WORLD, there are always certain groups of people who are treated like second-class citizens or like people who have fatal infectious diseases. Generally speaking, people who are different or who do not fit in tend to fall into this group: minorities, social misfits, scandalous sinners, and so forth. Favoritism is a universal sin. For various reasons, we love certain people but not all people. We are willing to befriend some folks but not others.

Yet, the Bible calls us to love all persons—not just those who love us, not just those who we like, and not just those who are like us. God wants us to love our enemies (Matt 5:43–45; Luke 10; Prov 25:21–22; Exod 23:4–5), the poor (Lev 19:9–10; Deut 15:11; Deut 24:19–21), the disabled (Lev 19:14), and the socially outcast (Lev 19:33–34).

In numerous places, the Bible forbids us from showing favoritism (Deut 10:17; Lev 19:15; 2 Chr 19:7; 1 Tim 5:21). For example, James 2:1 says, "My brothers, show no partiality." We are not to show favoritism because God himself is not partial, and we are to imitate our Father in heaven (Rom 2:11; Acts 10:34; Eph 6:9).

A Portrait of Christ

Loving all persons without favoritism is eminently displayed in the life of our Lord Jesus Christ. We see him loving and befriending the rich and the poor, the saint and the sinner, the popular and the unpopular, the important and unimportant, men and women, children and adults, Jew and Gentile. Now this does not mean that Jesus, as a man, did not have intimate friends. We can't be best friends with everyone. There are going to be people, for various reasons, that we click with and naturally knit our hearts to in affectionate friendship. Jesus is no exception to this very human phenomenon. Among the twelve disciples, Jesus developed a closer relationship to three: Peter, James, and John. And among these three, Jesus bonded most closely with John. Of the many friends he had outside of the twelve disciples, Mary, Martha, and especially Lazarus stand out (John 11).

That Jesus loved and befriended all types of persons also does not mean that he did not make a separation between those who loved God and those who didn't. Spiritual bonds are much stronger than even familial bonds. A special and eternal relationship exists between all believers, and all believers with the Lord Jesus. Hence, Jesus could say that whoever does the will of God is his brother or sister (Mark 3:35; Matt 12:5), and those who do the things that he commands are his friends (John 15:14).

Nevertheless, Jesus reached out to all sorts of people. He did not show favoritism to one or several groups of people. He did not stick to his friends, or if you will, to his "Christian friends." Now it is true that we need to be careful in choosing our good or best friends. The Bible clearly warns us that friends have the power to influence us for good or ill. So we must not hang out with unbelievers in order to be accepted by them or to be like them. Yet, we are to love all people, including unbelievers who desperately

Christ the Friend

need to be saved. For this is what we see our Lord Jesus doing in the Gospels. In order to see that this is the case, we are going to look at various snapshots from the life of Jesus to see how he interacted with all sorts of people. As we do so, two points should be kept in mind. First, by his example, Jesus teaches us how to concretely obey God's command to love all people. Second, that Jesus reaches out to all means that all are invited to come and be saved. It doesn't matter who you are, how strange you are, how much of an outsider you are, how rich or poor you are, or how much of a sinner you are, you are invited to come to Jesus. If you come humbly, seeking mercy, then you will find it. Whoever comes to Jesus will never be cast out (John 6:37).

Jesus and Covenant Children

The famous children's hymn "Jesus Loves Me" teaches that Jesus loves children, and that we know this because the Bible tells us so. But where does the Bible tell us Jesus loves little children? Mark 10:13–16 is one such place. In this passage, we see Jesus interacting with covenant children (children of the church). Parents (or their guardians) brought their children to see Jesus so that he might bless them. The disciples, however, rebuked the parents for doing so. We are not told the reason the disciples forbade them, but probably it was because they thought that Jesus was too important or too busy to see little children. When Jesus saw what his disciples were doing, he was indignant.

Have you had someone misrepresent your opinion or belief so that you were portrayed as holding to something that you utterly despise? This is what the disciples did with Jesus. By their actions, they were saying that Jesus did not care about children. Undoubtedly, the disciples were not doing this on purpose. They probably were thinking that they were doing Jesus a favor. But in so doing, they were not properly representing Jesus. And this made Jesus mad. Consequently, Jesus rebuked his disciples and commanded them to let the children come to him. He then held the children in his arms and blessed them.

What makes us angry reveals our character as well as what we think is important. The fact that Jesus was upset with his disciples teaches us that he delights in children and that they are very important to him. Jesus loves the little children.

Jesus and Scandalous Sinners

In Mark 2:13-17 (see also Matt 9:9-13; Luke 5:27-32), Jesus went to the home of Levi the tax collector, whom Jesus had recently called to be one of his disciples. Levi invited many of his friends to come and meet Jesus, and they all sat down together around the table, an act which symbolized friendship in that day and culture. Undoubtedly, everyone had a great time, with the sound of laughter filling the house.

Levi was a tax collector, and so of course many of his friends were tax collectors. Tax collectors were despised by their fellow Jews. All the nasty jokes of the day would have been at the tax collector's expense.

The tax system in Jesus' day was regulated, but it was a system that fostered fraud and dishonesty. Tax collectors had the power to stop someone on the road, make him unpack his bundles, and determine the amount of tax to be paid.[1] With this kind of power up for grabs, these positions were highly coveted, at least by a certain sleazy section of the population.[2] Since they were awarded to the highest

---

1 Hughes, *Mark*, 1:68.

2 Ibid.

Christ the Friend

bidder, it took a good deal of money to become a tax collector.[3] But it is not like any of them lost their investment. They often charged much more than was necessary, and so increased their own wealth at the expense of the tax-burdened citizen. And of course, if the person could not pay, the tax collector would offer to loan the money at an inflated rate.[4]

Eventually, the name "tax collector" became proverbial for lack of character and respect. They were often grouped together with brothel owners: tax collectors and pimps![5] Dishonesty was so characteristic of tax collectors that a Roman writer said he once saw a monument to an honest tax collector.[6] Add to this the fact that tax collectors cooperated with the Roman Empire, and it becomes clear why every Jew hated them.[7] As a result, they could not serve as judges or as witnesses in a Jewish court and they were excommunicated from the synagogues.[8]

So a bunch of these undesirables were having lunch with Jesus. But that is not all. Verse 16 says that he was also eating with "sinners." The term "sinner" could refer to immoral people like prostitutes, or to those who did not take the faith very seriously (nominal Jews), including those who did not follow the rituals and regulations of the Pharisees. "Sinners" were considered religious and social outcasts.

Here, then, was Jesus associating with scandalous sinners and social outcasts. To paint the picture with a contemporary brush: Jesus was befriending homosexuals, transvestites, and abortion doctors. He was enjoying lunch

3 Schmidt, "Taxes," 806.
4 Hughes, *Mark*, 1:68.
5 Schmidt, "Taxes," 805.
6 Hughes, *Mark*, 1:68.
7. Schmidt, "Taxes," 806; see also Hughes, *Mark*, 1:68.
8. Hughes, *Mark*, 1:69.

with them in a public restaurant, talking and laughing with them.

The Pharisees were greatly offended that Jesus did this and thought he was in the wrong. To eat with such people was contrary to the traditions that had been handed down and it created ritual impurity. This is why they asked Jesus' disciples in an accusatory manner, "Why does he eat with tax collectors and sinners?" (Mark 2:16). Also, in Luke 15:2, after noticing that the tax collectors and sinners were all drawing near to hear Jesus, the Pharisees and the scribes grumbled, saying, "This man receives sinners and eats with them."

There is an element of truth to the concern of the scribes and Pharisees. The Bible does warn the godly against befriending wicked people. Paul notes that bad company ruins good morals (1 Cor 15:33) and exhorts believers to not be yoked with unbelievers (2 Cor 6:14–18). Similarly, Solomon says, "Make no friendship with a man given to anger, nor go with a wrathful man" (Prov 22:24; see also Prov 16:29). Since the Bible exhorts the righteous to be separate from the unrighteous, how then can Jesus befriend "sinners" and "tax collectors"?

Jesus defends his actions in Luke 15 by telling three parables: the Lost Coin, the Lost Sheep, and the Prodigal Son. In Mark 2, Jesus' response is given in verse 17: "Those who are well have no need of a physician, but those who are sick. I came not to call the righteous, but sinners." Jesus did not spend time with the immoral in order to be like them or join their gang. He befriended them to call them to repentance and to urge them to enter the kingdom of God. What if a doctor refused to have anything to do with the sick? It would be ridiculous! Likewise, it would be just as ridiculous, if not more so, for the savior of sinners to not be the friend of sinners.

Christ the Friend

Jesus and the Self-Righteous

Sometimes it is easier to show the love of Christ to scandalous sinners, like prostitutes and drug addicts, than it is to the proud and self-righteous. Public sinners tend not to look down their noses on you. They don't want to be judged themselves, and so they do not judge others.

The proud and self-righteous, however, are blind to their pride and self-righteousness. They, therefore, tend to be judgmental and faultfinders. Slow to praise, quick to condemn. By tearing other people down and then using them as a yardstick, they can make themselves look good. People like this also tend to have their own set of rules by which they judge other people. But even if they use God's law as a standard (or if they think their rules are God's rules), they often focus only on the part that they are good at keeping. That way they still look good, while others still fall short. People like this tend to be harsh, unforgiving, unyielding, and judgmental. And, quite frankly, they are hard to live with.

I remember one time hearing a sermon on the tax collector and the Pharisee (Luke 18). As the preacher described the Pharisee, it became obvious how terrible the Pharisee was, and I began to be glad that I was not like him. But then at the end of the sermon, the preacher pointed out that what I was thinking was in fact no different from the Pharisee! The Pharisee was glad he was not like the tax collector, just as I was glad I was not the Pharisee.

What the tax collector was in Jesus' day, the Pharisee is in our own day. In Jesus' day, the Pharisees were regarded as outstanding saints, paragons of virtue. We, and rightly so, do not see them that way, because the New Testament clearly tells us that they were self-righteous hypocrites. Hence, to call someone a Pharisee today is an insult. But of course the Pharisee (the self-righteous, judgmental sinner) needs the gospel just as much as the prostitute and drug addict. Pharisees need to be loved and befriended, too, which is exactly what we see Jesus doing in the Gospels. He not only reached out to tax collectors and sinners. He also sought out Pharisees. In Luke 7:36–50, Jesus went to a Pharisee's house to eat with him, while in John 3, he entertained Nicodemus's late-night call. Moreover, by means of the parable of the Prodigal Son, Jesus lovingly pleaded with the Pharisees to repent of their sins.[9] Thus, the Lord "is not a Pharisee about Pharisees; he is not self-righteous about self-righteousness . . . he not only loves the wild-living, free-spirited people, but also hardened religious people."[10]

Jesus and the Samaritan Woman

In John 4, Jesus met and conversed with a Samaritan woman. What is striking about this is that from a cultural standpoint she had three strikes against her. First, she was a woman. John 4:27 says that the disciples were shocked that Jesus was talking to a woman. This is because women were often regarded as second class citizens. Second, she was a Samaritan. Jews and Samaritans hated each other. They were mortal enemies. Most Jews would walk around Samaria in order to avoid having to go through Samaria. Third, she was an immoral woman. She had been married five times, and the man she was currently living with was not her husband.

Yet, Jesus sat down with her, started up a conversation, and led her to embrace the truth. Jesus loved and befriended her. When he looked at her, he didn't see a

9. See Keller, *Prodigal God*, 74.
10. Keller, *Prodigal God*, 74–75.

Christ the Friend

woman, a Samaritan, or a scandalous sinner. What he saw was a person made in the image of God, a person worthy of respect, dignity, and love. He saw a person in desperate need of the savior.

God is not partial. Therefore Jesus is not partial. When he lived here on earth, he reached out to all peoples, regardless of their status, lifestyle, age, sex, or race. Jesus loves sinners. Jesus befriends sinners. He is the savior of sinners. So follow Jesus by becoming his disciple, because he will certainly accept you (John 6:37).

6

The Anger of Christ

HAVE YOU EVER KNOWN someone that was extremely kind and compassionate? Nothing, or seemingly nothing, upset him, and he always took everything in stride. But then one day you see him fly off the handle or say something so out of character that you are in utter shock. You see a side of your friend that you never knew existed.

We tend to think of Jesus as someone who is gentle, mild, and caring. He wouldn't hurt a fly, as the saying goes. Now as we have seen, Jesus is all of these things. He is truly compassionate and gentle. As Isaiah so eloquently put it, "He will not cry aloud or lift up his voice, or make it heard in the street; a bruised reed he will not break, and a faintly burning wick he will not quench" (Isa 42:2–3). But the Gospels also teach us that there is another side to Jesus. He is meek and humble, but he is also great and powerful. He is loving and compassionate, but he is also angry and wrathful. He is highly approachable, but he is also to be feared. He is a lamb and also a lion. James Stewart captured this truth about Jesus quite well when he said:

> [Jesus] was the meekest and lowliest of all the sons of men, yet he spoke of coming on the

> clouds of heaven with the glory of God. He was so austere that evil spirits and demons cried out in terror at his coming, yet he was so genial and winsome and approachable that the children loved to play with him, and the little ones nestled in his arms. His presence at the innocent gaiety of a village wedding was like the presence of sunshine.
>
> No one was half so compassionate to sinners, yet no one ever spoke such red hot, scorching words about sin. A bruised reed he would not break. His whole life was love, yet on one occasion he demanded of the Pharisees how they ever expected to escape the damnation of hell. He was a dreamer of dreams and a seer of visions, yet for sheer stark realism he has all of us self-styled realists soundly beaten. He was a servant of all, washing the disciples' feet, yet masterfully he strode into the temple, and the hucksters and moneychangers fell over one another from the mad rush and the fire they saw blazing in his eyes.
>
> He saved others, yet at the last, himself he did not save. There is nothing in history like the union of contrasts that confronts us in the Gospels. The mystery of Jesus is the mystery of divine personality.[1]

If we are going to have a fuller understanding of Jesus, we need to consider more than one facet of his life. Having looked at the loving side, we want to turn our attention to the angry, wrathful side. On numerous occasions, Jesus got angry. In his anger, he both spoke and acted very sternly.

---

1. Quoted by Zacharias, *Has Christianity Failed You?*, 28.

A Portrait of Christ

As we look at some of the occasions that Jesus got angry, we need to keep in mind two things. First, as God, Jesus reveals God to us. The mystery of Jesus is the mystery of divine personality. God is not only a God of love, he is also a consuming fire (Heb 12:29). In Romans 11:22, Paul says, "Note then the kindness and the severity of God." We have seen the kindness of God displayed in Christ, and now we will see the severity of God exemplified in Christ.

The second thing to keep in mind is that as a man, Jesus is an example to us. The fact that Jesus gets upset teaches us that anger is not necessarily wrong. It is sinful to be angry without cause or for the wrong reasons. Moreover, we must be careful not to sin in our anger. But it is not wrong to be angry. In fact, it would be wrong not to be angry when we should be angry! The sight of wickedness and cruelty, for example, should make us furious. After all, we are moral beings created in the image of God. To not react this way, therefore, would be to go against our created nature. Thus, it really should not surprise anyone to see fire blazing in Jesus' eyes when he is confronted with evil.

Jesus Cleanses the Temple

There are several accounts of Jesus cleansing the temple (Matt 21:12–17; Mark 11:15–19; Luke 19:45–48; John 2:13–22). We will use John 2:13–22 as the basis for our exposition.

It was the time for the Passover, so Jesus went to Jerusalem. John tells us that when Jesus arrived at the temple he found merchants and money changers conducting their business. The merchants were there to provide people with animals for sacrifices. Hence, they sold oxen, sheep, and doves. This was a convenient service, especially for those who traveled from afar. The money changers also provided

The Anger of Christ

a helpful service. The temple tax had to be paid with a certain coinage. Many who came did not have that coinage and thus needed to change their currency.

These merchants and money changers conducted their business in the outer court of the temple, that is, the court of the Gentiles. This practice of doing business in the outer court of the temple was approved by the temple authorities.[2] It was not deemed unusual by the people.

Although it was an acceptable practice to the priests, it was completely unacceptable to Jesus. Out of consuming zeal—that is, in righteous anger—he made a whip out of cords and used it to drive the sheep and oxen out of the temple. He poured out the money changers' money on the ground and overturned their tables. To those who sold doves, he told them to take them away.

Why did Jesus do this? What made him so angry? It was not necessarily because these merchants and money changers were taking advantage of the people. After all, the people were not forced to exchange their money or buy their animals at the temple. The commercial practice itself was not wrong. It was where they did it that was so wrong. They conducted their business in the temple. By doing so, they perverted the worship of God, and prevented the Gentiles from worshipping in the temple. Hence, Jesus said, "Do not make My Father's house a house of trade" (John 2:16).

The temple was where the faithful went to meet with God. They went there to pray, to worship, to offer sacrifices, and so forth. But now it had been turned into a market place, and that made Jesus burn with fury.

---

2. Carson, *John*, 178–79.

A Portrait of Christ

Jesus and the Scribes and Pharisees

In Mark 3, Jesus entered a synagogue, where there happened to be a man who had a withered hand. The Pharisees watched Jesus closely to see if he would heal the man on the Sabbath day, in order to accuse him. The Pharisees believed that healing was only proper on the Sabbath if it was a life and death situation. This man's life was not in danger, and so they believed he should not be healed on the Sabbath.

Jesus told the man with the withered hand to come to him. Then he said to the Pharisees, "Is it lawful on the Sabbath to do good or to do harm, to save life or to kill?" (Mark 3:4). On a different, but similar, occasion, Jesus asked the Pharisees, "Which of you, having a son or an ox that has fallen into a well on a Sabbath day, will not immediately pull him out?" (Luke 14:5).

There was a deafening silence to Jesus' question on both occasions. They had no answer. Jesus had deftly exposed their double standard and their perverted view of the Sabbath. But what is more, he had uncovered their insensitivity to human suffering. They were more concerned about their ridiculous rules than the welfare of a fellow human being. They would help their animal on a Sabbath, but they did not want human suffering to be alleviated on the Sabbath.

In response to this sinfulness and cruelty, Mark 3:5 says, "And he looked around at them with anger." Jesus was indignant at the Pharisees for the way they treated their fellow human beings. Interestingly, the Pharisees became angry at Jesus. Luke's account of this same event tells us that after Jesus healed the man, "they were filled with fury and discussed with one another what they might do to Jesus" (Luke 6:11). Mark adds that they got together with the Herodians to discuss how they might kill Jesus. In Jesus, we

The Anger of Christ

have an example of righteous anger, and in the Pharisees, we have an example of unrighteous, sinful anger.

In Matthew 23, Jesus said some very harsh things to and about the scribes and Pharisees. He did not hesitate to call them "hypocrites," "blind guides," "whitewashed tombs," and "brood of vipers." The Lord even uttered curses against them: "Woe to you, scribes and Pharisees..." This he did because of their unrepentant wickedness: cruelty, pride, terrible teaching and practice, damnable heresy, leading of others to hell, hypocrisy, lawbreaking, and persecution of the righteous. Elsewhere, Jesus referred to them as "ravenous wolves" and even children of the devil (Matt 7:15; John 8:44).

Further Examples of Jesus' Anger

Jesus' anger and stern words, however, were not only directed toward the scribes and Pharisees. He called Herod "that fox" (Luke 13:32) and likened the unreceptive or thickheaded to pigs (Matt 7:6).

In the parable of the Ten Minas, Jesus portrayed himself as a judge, saying to his enemies, "But as for these enemies of mine who did not want me to reign over them, bring them here and slaughter them before me" (Luke 19:27). This is reminiscent of Psalm 2, which is a messianic psalm, and thus speaks of Jesus. Verse 12 says, "Kiss the Son, lest he be angry, and you perish in the way, for his wrath is quickly kindled."

We should also note that Jesus' anger is not limited to unbelievers and hypocrites. Jesus was terribly upset with his own disciples for keeping the children from coming to him (Mark 10:13–16). In Mark 8, Jesus spoke very harshly to Peter. After instructing his disciples about his impending death at the hands of those who often made him angry,

A Portrait of Christ

Jesus was rebuked by Peter, who might have said something like this: "There is no way you are going to die! You are the Messiah, the Son of God, as I have just confessed! You yourself said I was right and that God himself has revealed this to me! So of course you are not going to die!" Peter immediately found out that he had put his foot in his mouth. For Jesus turned and rebuked him, saying, "Get behind me, Satan! For you are not setting your mind on the things of God, but on the things of man" (Mark 8:33). Peter was tempting Jesus to disobey God, and so received a harsh rebuke.

Another interesting episode in the life of Jesus is found in John 11. This chapter recounts the death and subsequent resurrection of Lazarus. When Jesus saw Mary and the Jews who were with her weeping, verse 33 says that Jesus was "deeply moved in his spirit." The NKJV says, "he groaned." The word used here refers to the "snorting of horses." When applied to humans it means anger, outrage, or emotional indignation. Hence, the NLT says, "a deep anger welled up within him." Jesus was outraged at death. He is furious at the wages of sin that plague his people and undoubtedly at the one who has (or rather had) the power of death, Satan.

Based upon these examples, then, B. B. Warfield is quite correct to conclude that "Jesus burned with anger against the wrongs he met with in his journey through human life as truly as he melted with pity at the sight of the world's misery."[3]

Sadly, people can be extremely mean and cruel to each other. It is rather amazing what people do to other people. Indeed, it is terrible what Christians do to each other. Wickedness, at times, runs rampant in this world. But what does God think about these things? How does God react when we sin against each other and when evil things happen in this world?

3. Warfield, "Emotional Life," 67.

The Anger of Christ

Well, we do not have to guess the answer. We know that God is furious with sinners over their sin, because that is how Jesus, the Son of God, reacted to sinners in their sin. We should never conclude from the fact that God is love and full of compassion that he turns a blind eye to our wickedness and cruelty. He is not like a big old teddy bear, gentle and nice to everyone, regardless of what they do. God hates sin and sinners (Ps 5:5). It is a fearful thing to fall into the hands of the living God (Heb 10:31).

In the book *The Lion, the Witch and the Wardrobe*, Lucy asks Mr. Beaver if Aslan the Lion is safe. Mr. Beaver replies, "Safe? 'Course he isn't safe. But he's good."[4] Jesus is good, kind, and compassionate. But he is not safe. He is not safe to those who rebel against him and who remain in their sin. Note, then, the kindness and the severity of the Lord Jesus Christ.

---

4. Lewis, *The Lion, the Witch and the Wardrobe*, 86.

7

The Humility of Christ

ALTHOUGH HE IS THE Son of God, Jesus is a human in every respect, except without sin. This is not to say that God the Son took over or meshed with a human person, so that Jesus has a divine person and a human person. Rather, the person of Jesus is the Son of God and he has two natures: divine and human. As a man, without sin, he was perfect. The life he lived here on earth, therefore, was an exemplary life. In Jesus, we see how a human being is to act and live before God and before other human beings.

There is one characteristic or attribute that I think nicely sums up the kind of life Jesus lived here on earth. Interestingly enough, it is the one character trait that Jesus himself mentioned he had. He brought attention to it, at least in part, because of its attractiveness and appeal. A person who exhibits this trait is someone you can befriend, and follow. He is like a breath of fresh air, pleasant and nice. But a person who has the opposite characteristic is annoying, harsh, and very unappealing. He makes you want to turn your back and run in the opposite direction. Jesus wants people to come to him so that they might find rest, salvation, and life. And in order to encourage people to come to him, he told them that he has this attractive attribute.

What is this attribute or character trait? It is humility, or lowliness of heart, which is closely associated with meekness and gentleness. Matthew 11:29: "Take my yoke upon you, and learn from me, for I am gentle and lowly in heart, and you will find rest for your souls."

In Micah 6:8, the prophet sums up our duty to God: "He has told you, O man, what is good; and what does the LORD require of you but to do justice, and to love kindness, and to walk humbly with your God?" Here is an apt description of Jesus' life. He was just, loved kindness, and walked humbly before God and man.

The Lord's humble life is something that we are called upon to emulate. As Peter says, the Lord left us an example, so that we might follow in his steps (1 Pet 2:21). So as we look at concrete examples of the Lord's humility, keep in mind that we are to go and do likewise. But before we do this, let us first briefly define humility.

What is Humility?

Humility involves a proper assessment of oneself before God. Paul says that we should not think of ourselves more highly than we ought to think, but to think with sober judgment (Rom 12:3). On the one hand, humility is not thinking less of yourself and the gifts, abilities, and roles that God has given you. On the other hand, humility is not thinking more of yourself and the gifts, abilities, and roles that God has given you.

Hence, it was not arrogant for Jesus to make the claim that he was the Son of God, the Messiah, or that people should honor him even as they honor the Father (John

A Portrait of Christ

5:23). The scribes and Pharisees, of course, thought he was blasphemously proud, and so deserving of death (John 5:18; 19:7).

But Jesus was not claiming anything that was not true and that was not supported with ample evidence. The Father himself testified who Jesus was at his baptism. Further support came from the testimony of John the Baptist, Jesus' miracles, and the Scriptures.

The author of Hebrews says that no one takes the honor of being a priest for himself. He can only do so when called by God, just as Aaron was (Heb 5:4). Those who tried to take this honor for themselves were punished by God in the Old Testament. Jesus did not arrogantly take it upon himself to be the great high priest. Rather, as the author of Hebrews says, he was appointed to this role by God (Heb 5:5–10).

So it was not arrogant for Jesus to make the claim that he was the Christ and that he was the Son of God. Indeed, he was only doing and saying what the Father wanted him to do and say (John 5:30; 12:49–50). Moreover, Jesus did not carry out his divinely appointed role in an arrogant manner. He did not go around boasting he was the Messiah and sticking it in people's faces. He said what he said and did what he did humbly, in response to challenges by the Pharisees, to draw people to himself and to please his Father in heaven.

Humility also involves submission to God. At or near the center of the biblical meaning of humility is submission and obedience to God (Jas 4:6–7; 1 Pet 5:5). A humble person knows his place before God. He acknowledges that he is but the Lord's servant and readily submits to the Lord's will. Mary beautifully demonstrated humility when she said to the angel Gabriel, upon hearing the news that she would

The Humility of Christ

become pregnant, "Behold, I am the servant of the Lord; let it be to me according to your word" (Luke 1:38).

By contrast, the proud and arrogant shake their fist at God (see Ezek 16:49–50). Although they may have the image of godliness, in the end they do what they want to do and not what God commands them to do. It is sometimes said, and rightly so, that the root of all sin is pride: a desire to be like God and the judge of right and wrong.

The proud, therefore, do not hesitate to claim an authority or right that does not belong to them. When Uzziah became strong, 2 Chronicles 26:16 says, "he grew proud, to his destruction." In his pride, he strode into the temple to burn incense, something only the priest was allowed to do. The king was confronted by Azariah the priest, but this only made him angry. The Lord then struck the king with leprosy, which he had till the day he died. Similarly, the Bible says that Pharaoh was arrogant in the way he treated Israel, and that in refusing to let Israel go, he was refusing to humble himself before the Lord (Neh 9:10; Exod 10:3).

Still further, humility involves counting others more significant than ourselves. In terms of our horizontal relationships, humility expresses itself in giving up our own rights and serving others. Paul says in Philippians 2:3–4, "Do nothing from rivalry or conceit, but in humility count others more significant than yourselves. Let each of you look not only to his own interests, but also to the interests of others."

Instead of looking down on other people, a humble person looks up. He is willing to sit at the back of the bus or give up his turn so that someone else can play the game. He is gentle and kind, not boastful, stuck up, condescending, or selfish.

Humility, however, is not the same thing as humiliation or weakness. To be humble is a good thing, while to be humiliated is not good at all. True humility is not a "lay-down-and-walk-all-over-me-whenever-anyone-feels-like-it" disposition. Nor is it to be equated with cowardliness, timidity, or a shy, soft-spoken personality.

Apparently, Timothy was a timid, reserved person by nature. His timidity was even getting in the way of his ministry, so at one point Paul encouraged him to be more assertive by saying, "For God gave us a spirit not of fear but of power and love and self-control" (2 Tim 1:7). Here we see that a spirit of fear and timidity is not from the Holy Spirit. And therefore humility is not contrary to courage, confidence, boldness, and strength.

The truth of the matter is that one can be full of courage and strength and yet be humble through and through. Once again, we see the union of contrasts that is found in Jesus. He was great, powerful, courageous, and confident. Yet, he was also the most humble man to walk on the face of the earth. This is true with respect to his relationship with the Father in heaven and other human beings.

Jesus' Humility before God

Humility before God expresses itself in submission and obedience, which is what we see dominating the life of our Lord. In John 4:34, Jesus says, "my food is to do the will of him who sent me and to accomplish his work." Jesus, of course, is not saying that he doesn't need to eat or drink. What he is saying is that there is a greater sustenance and satisfaction in doing God's will than that which is provided by food. Pleasing God is more important and more fulfilling than anything else, including food when one is hungry and drink when one is thirsty.

Jesus' chief end, then, was to glorify God. Doing the will of God was like food to him: delightful and satisfying

The Humility of Christ

(Ps 40:8; Ps 119:24, 35, 47, 72, 77, 93, 129). On numerous occasions, Jesus expressed his consuming desire to obey God. Indeed, that was the very reason he came down from heaven: "For I have come down from heaven, not to do my own will but the will of him who sent me" (John 6:38) and "I do as the Father has commanded me, so that the world may know that I love the Father" (John 14:31).

After Jesus fed the five thousand, the people were amazed, believing that he was the prophet that was to come into the world. They therefore decided to make him their king. Seeing that the people were intent on doing this, Jesus quietly escaped to the mountain by himself. Here we see that true humility is not the same thing as people pleasing. Jesus' number one goal was to submit to the Father. The people, however, wanted to make him their king in a way that was contrary to the Father's will. And they were not going to take no for an answer. Jesus could have easily appealed to the crowd and won their approval by succumbing to their desires. Instead of seeking glory from men, he sought to glorify his Father in heaven (John 5:41).

What did the Father want Jesus to do? Why did he send Jesus down from heaven? It was to save his people from their sins. It was to die and rise again from the dead so that "everyone who looks on the Son and believes in him should have eternal life" and be raised up on the last day (John 6:40). Although it caused him incredible suffering in mind, body, and soul, Jesus submitted to the Father's will. Hence, Paul wrote that Jesus humbled himself by becoming obedient to the point of death, even death on a cross (Phil 2:8). The humble one is the obedient one, and the obedient one is the humble one.

A Portrait of Christ

Jesus' Humility before People

Zechariah the prophet foretold that the messianic king would be humble and mounted on a donkey (Zechariah 9). Riding on a donkey, instead of a grand war horse, was a visible picture of humility. So when Jesus entered Jerusalem the week of his death, he rode into Jerusalem on a donkey, in fulfillment of this prophecy, but also to symbolize his lowliness of heart.

Jesus also demonstrated his humility when he stooped down to wash his disciples' feet (John 13). People in those days wore sandals. Walking on dirt roads naturally caused their feet to become quite filthy. It was customary, therefore, to wash or to have your feet washed upon entering a home. Hosts would supply a basin of water and a towel for guests to wash their feet. The wealthy would have a slave perform this task, but only a Gentile slave. Jewish servants were not required to do this, because it was considered too demeaning.[1] Hence, when Jesus, a superior, got down on his knees before Peter, it was simply too much for the outspoken disciple, and he strongly objected.

Although he is the Son of God and the son of David (and thus of royal blood, humanly speaking), Jesus rode on a donkey and washed his disciples' feet. These two events were but a reflection of his whole life and of the work he came to do. Jesus said, "For even the Son of Man came not to be served but to serve, and to give his life as a ransom for many" (Mark 10:45).

Jesus came to save us by dying for our sins and being raised again from the dead for our justification. He had to humble himself so that we might be exalted. That is why he rode on a donkey, not a war horse. He came to lay down his life, and not take up the sword, like David. That is why he

---

1. Köstenburger, *John*, 405.

The Humility of Christ

insisted on washing Peter's feet. We need Jesus to wash us, not the other way around. And until Jesus washes us, we remain unclean.

Paul put it this way, in 2 Corinthians 8:9: "For you know the grace of our Lord Jesus Christ, that though he was rich, yet for your sake he became poor, so that you by his poverty might become rich." The Son of God gave up the glories of heaven to come down to earth and take on humanity in order to save us. He humbled himself. And he not only humbled himself, he allowed himself to be humiliated, killed, and cursed by God. He came not to be served but to serve.

Sometimes it is easy to be humble when you are not in a position of strength or power. It is easier to submit when you know that resistance is futile. By the same token, it is easy to be assertive, selfish, and demanding when you are in the position of physical or moral strength. If we have the right to something, we can be quick to demand that others satisfy that right. When we are in a position of authority, we can be quick to wield that authority to do and to get what we want.

Jesus did not have to come to earth. He didn't have to die, because he was perfectly righteous. He said that no one took his life, but that he laid it down of his own accord (John 10:18). Even Satan had no claim on Jesus (John 14:30). John's account of Jesus' betrayal, arrest, trial, and death shows us that the Lord was in complete control of everything that was happening. He was far from a helpless victim. In fact, Jesus told his disciples during his arrest that he could have appealed to his Father, who would have then sent to his defense more than twelve legions of angels (Matt 26:54).

So Jesus was in complete control. Nevertheless, he gave up his rights and refused to exercise his authority to save himself, in order to save his people from their sins. He not only looked out for his own interests, but also to the interests of others.

Throughout this series on the life of Christ, we have emphasized that Jesus is God the Son with two natures: divine and human. He is therefore fully God and fully man. Consequently, we have emphasized two things about Jesus' life. First, as a man, Jesus' life is an example for us to emulate. And second, as God, Jesus' life displays the divine nature. The humility of Christ is not only an example for us to follow (Philippians 2), it is also a revelation of the character of God.

God is great and holy, and yet he humbles himself to care for his creation. He stoops down to fellowship with, to provide for, and even to save humankind. This causes the psalmist to exclaim in amazement, "What is man that you are mindful of him, and the son of man that you care for him?" (Ps 8:4; see also Ps 113:5–6). God is not proud or arrogant. He is good, gentle, kind, and humble. Jesus is proof. So come to Jesus and taste and see that the LORD is good! Blessed is the man who takes refuge in him (Ps 34:8)!

Bibliography

Bavinck, Herman. *Reformed Dogmatics*. Vol. 3, *Sin and Salvation in Christ*. Edited by John Bolt. Translated by John Vriend. Grand Rapids: Baker, 2006.

Bonar, Andrew A. *Memoir and Remains of Robert Murray M'Cheyne*. Carlisle, PA: Banner of Truth, 1987.

Carson, D. A. *The Gospel According to John*. Pillar New Testament Commentary. Grand Rapids: Eerdmans, 1991.

Committee on Christian Education of the Orthodox Presbyterian Church. *The Confession of Faith and Catechisms: The Westminster Confession of Faith and Catechisms as Adopted by the Orthodox Presbyterian Church; with Proof Texts*. Willow Grove, PA: Orthodox Presbyterian Church, 2005.

Grudem, Wayne. *Systematic Theology: An Introduction to Biblical Doctrine*. Grand Rapids: Zondervan, 1994.

Hughes, R. Kent. *Mark: Jesus, Servant and Savior*. 2 vols. Preaching the Word. Westchester, IL: Crossway, 1989.

Keller, Timothy J. *The Prodigal God: Recovering the Heart of the Christian Faith*. New York: Dutton, 2008.

Köstenberger, Andreas J. *John*. Baker Exegetical Commentary on the New Testament. Grand Rapids: Baker Academic, 2004.

Lewis, C. S. *The Lion, the Witch and the Wardrobe*. New York: HarperTrophy, 1978.

Manton, Thomas. "Sermon XVI." In *The Works of Thomas Manton, D. D.*, edited by Thomas Smith, 2:340–57. London: James Nisbet, 1871.

Palmer, Benjamin M. *Sermons of Rev. B. M. Palmer*. Harrisonburg, VA: Sprinkle, 2002.

Schmidt, T. E. "Taxes." In *Dictionary of Jesus and the Gospels*, edited by J. B. Green et al., 804–6. Downers Grove, IL: InterVarsity, 1992.

Bibliography

Warfield, B. B. "The Deity of Christ." In *Selected Shorter Writings of Benjamin B. Warfield*, edited by John E. Meeter, 1:151–57. Phillipsburg, NJ: Presbyterian and Reformed, 2001.

———. "On the Emotional Life of Our Lord." In *Biblical and Theological Studies by Members of the Faculty of Princeton Theological Seminary*, 35–90. New York: Scribner's, 1912.

Zacharias, Ravi. *Has Christianity Failed You?* Grand Rapids: Zondervan, 2010.

Study Guide

Chapter 1

1. In what ways do *The Lord of the Rings* and *The Lion, the Witch and the Wardrobe* reflect biblical truths? What are some other books or movies that reflect the same biblical truths?
2. What is the difference between God's providential kingdom and his redemptive kingdom?
3. How do the events surrounding the birth of Jesus demonstrate that he is the promised Christ?
4. How do Jesus' preaching, exorcisms, and miracles of healing prove that he is the promised Christ?
5. How does Jesus save his people from Satan, sin, and death?

Chapter 2

1. How do the Gospels demonstrate that Jesus is a normal human being?
2. Why does the savior have to be a normal human being?

Study Guide

3. How do the Gospels prove that Jesus is fully and completely divine?
4. Why does the savior have to be divine?
5. What are some incorrect ways of understanding the relationship between the humanity and divinity of Christ? What is the correct understanding?

Chapter 3

1. What two things does the life of Christ teach us?
2. What are some examples of Jesus' compassion that are discussed in this chapter?
3. Since Jesus is compassionate, why doesn't he immediately help people when they ask him in prayer?
4. How should Jesus' compassion toward people impact us?

Chapter 4

1. Does Jesus love all people equally?
2. How did Jesus take care of his disciples (especially Peter) and his mother during his own time of intense struggle?
3. How is Jesus' love for his people seen in his prayers for them?
4. What does it mean for Jesus to love his people "to the end"?
5. What is one of Satan's chief tactics to destroy a Christian's faith? How can a believer counteract this satanic attack?

Study Guide

Chapter 5

1. Is it wrong to make distinctions among friends?
2. What two things do we learn from the fact that Jesus reached out to everyone?
3. Why were the Pharisees angry at Jesus for eating with tax collectors and sinners? What element of truth were they using to accuse Jesus of sin? How did Jesus respond to the Pharisees' accusation?
4. What kind of person or group of people do you find hard to befriend?

Chapter 6

1. Are anger and wrath compatible with love, compassion, and gentleness?
2. What two things do we learn from the examples of Jesus' anger?
3. Why was Jesus angry when he cleansed the temple?
4. Why was Jesus angry with the Pharisees in Mark 3:1–6?
5. Is Jesus ever angry with Christians?
6. How should we respond to Jesus,' and thus to God's, anger?

Chapter 7

1. Why did Jesus tell people he was humble or lowly in heart?
2. What is humility?

Study Guide

3. Why wasn't it arrogant of Jesus to say that people should honor him as they honor the Father?
4. What are some events depicted in the Gospels that highlight Jesus' humility?
5. What truth makes Jesus' humility all the more remarkable?
6. What does Jesus' humility teach us about God?

www.ingramcontent.com/pod-product-compliance
Lightning Source LLC
Chambersburg PA
CBHW070326100426
42743CB00011B/2572